AS IT IS IN HEAVEN

Rob Rowe

Copyright © 2020 Rob Rowe

All rights reserved. No portion of this book may be reproduced or transmitted in any form by any means - electronic, mechanical, photocopy, recording, scanning, or other - except for brief quotations in reviews or articles, without the prior written permission of the author.

Executive Editor – Bryan Allain

And a huge thanks to Marlin Detweiler, Joe Lundy and Abby Henry for also contributing to the editing process

Find More From Rob Rowe online:

YouTube: Robby Rowe

Instagram: robrowe_g1

Scripture quotations are taken from the Amplified Bible unless otherwise noted.

Printed in the U.S.A.

AS IT IS IN HEAVEN

A Prayer for all who read

Father God, you know that my heart for this book is that it would encourage people, comfort people, and teach people the simplicity of Christianity and the power of Your Love. Please speak to their hearts and lead them into a deeper relationship with You and Your precious Son, Jesus.

Help us to better understand Your love for us and the life You've called us to live. In Jesus' Name, Amen.

A Note From The Author

How should you read this book? A few suggestions...

- Have your Bible (or Bible app) on hand to read some of the verses referenced. This book isn't meant to replace the Bible, but rather to get you to dive into it with a fresh perspective.

- Highlight/underline sentences that stick out to you.

- Once you're finished reading, go back and find the things that stuck out to you to read them again and to find the referenced verses in the Bible.

- I prefer the Amplified and New King James versions of the Bible. The Amplified helps define some of the words from the original Hebrew, Aramaic, and Greek languages.

Ultimately, this book is designed to...

- Help you build a foundation for your relationship with the Lord through simple, biblical truths.

* * *

- Equip you to live life to the fullest by showing you that your relationship with God and Jesus, through the Holy Spirit, is what matters most.

PART ONE

THE TREE

Chapter 1 - A Close Call

It all happened so fast, but for some reason the replay in my mind is in super slow motion.

There was my dog, Clark, darting across the street just moments after I had dropped his leash.

There was the black pickup truck that seemed to appear out of nowhere, barreling right toward him.

And then there was the old man, who, as far as I'm concerned, saved Clark's life.

I'm still not sure how they didn't both end up dead, but thinking back on the incident with what I know now, I have a theory.

By the time I'm done with this story, you just might believe it, too.

Chapter 2 - Breaking News

Just when I thought things couldn't get any worse, I see it flashing across the screen:

Breaking news: Governor shuts down school for remainder of the year.

Are you kidding me? The coronavirus pandemic keeps getting worse and it seems my life is following suit. School canceled. Sports canceled. Prom canceled. Hanging out with friends canceled. They might as well just go ahead and cancel fun and smiling while they're at it.

The Stay-At-Home Order they issued earlier in the month has kept us stuck in the house, except for runs to get the essential stuff like groceries, gas, or medicine. That's probably the toughest part of this whole thing; being stuck here with two parents that seem to be going crazy. I wish they could just chill, but they walk around the house full of stress, worry, and tons of fear. It feels like they are paranoid about everything.

With them both being laid off, it's constant 24/7 craziness here. If they're not watching the news, they're talking about the virus. And when they run out of things to talk about, they just turn the news back on. Honestly, the only thing that's been keeping me sane so far is taking our pup, Clark, on walks.

And as if all of that wasn't bad enough, I'm still dealing with the grief of losing my grandfather last month. He and I had become really close over the last couple of years and I miss him so much. My parents are always working, so he was always at the house. He took me everywhere: to school, friends' houses, sports practices and games, out to eat, and church. You name it, we did it.

He passed away in the middle of his sleep, which, according to the doctors is a peaceful way to go. But, peaceful or not, I can't believe he's gone and I'm not sure how I'm supposed to get through all this without him, especially when the only thing you can do these days is sit around and think.

I can hear my parents in the other room arguing about whether or not grocery stores should be checking customer's temperatures, so this seems like the perfect time to take Clark back out. At least when I'm outside I can get away from everyone reminding me how much my life sucks. I put the pup on the leash and head for the door.

"Taking Clark out for a walk," I say as I step outside.

"BE CAREFUL!" My mom yells back, as the door closes behind me. "And remember, SOCIAL DISTANCING!"

I roll my eyes and wonder if Clark is rolling his, too.

The weather is gorgeous today. 55 degrees, a slight breeze,

and not a cloud in the sky. Spring flowers are beginning to bloom in everyone's landscaping, and it seems like half the neighborhood is outside working in their yards because, I mean, what else is there do?

Clark seems just as happy as I am to get out of that toxic house. He's such an awesome dog. He's a brindle boxer so he has that "tiger" look to him. Five years old and 87 lbs, the old boy is a hunk of love, tons of sloppy kisses, and plenty of snuggle time on the couch. My favorite part about him is his white socks and big, white fur chest.

I try to get my mind off of everything going on as we head away from the house, but it feels like the negative thoughts are following me. It's hard to think of anything else. Life just flat out sucks right now. No friends, no prom, no sports, and I can't even go to school. I used to complain about school, but now I just wish I could go and be with my friends.

I just want my life back, but all I'm hearing around me is how bad things are and how they're getting worse. People are dying, other countries have locked down all of their citizens, and New York City is on total shut down. I don't usually get freaked out about this kind of stuff, but this is really scary.

"Really great senior year," I mumble under my breath, but as I do, I accidentally let Clark's leash go and just like that, he's racing away from me.

"Hey come back!" I scream, sprinting after him down the sidewalk. I assume he's headed toward the church field where we've played catch once or twice before. I'm pretty fast, but even at full speed I'm not gonna catch him.

* * *

But then, just as he's about to get to the field, he takes a hard left between two parked cars and darts into the street. "No!" I yell, and as I do, I see the truck. It's no more than thirty feet from where Clark darted out and probably going fifteen over the speed limit.

"STOP!!!" I scream, sprinting up the sidewalk. Because of all the parked cars I can't see Clark, but seconds later I hear screeching tires. I cringe, bracing myself for whatever sound I'm about to hear. It's three seconds that feel like three minutes. But the screeching stops a moment later without any thud or crash.

I wedge myself between two parked cars and out into the street, and what I see stops me in my tracks. Clark is standing there, about five feet in front of the bumper of the black truck. And beside him is an old man, probably in his eighties, facing the truck with both arms over his head. How the car didn't hit both of them I do not understand, considering how fast it was going.

I'm frozen in my tracks, but Clark sees me and he comes running over. The couple in the pickup truck drive around the old man and give me dirty looks for the near-miss as they pass by. I can't believe Clark is okay.

"Well, that was close," the old man says, slowly walking over to us.

"I'm so sorry, sir," I say between gulps of breath. "I didn't mean to let him go. I guess I wasn't paying attention and he just slipped out of my hands. I don't even know what just happened. How did you…where did you…"

* * *

"No worries, son!" The old guy says with a smile. "Just didn't want to see Clark hurt. Happy to see that he's okay!"

"Wait, what?" I say, turning my confused eyes from the pup to the old guy.

"How do you know Clark's name?"

Chapter 3 - A New Friend

The old man laughs and looks up at me with a kind smile.

"I know who Clark is and I'm pretty sure I know who you are, too. You're Harold's grandson, right? Your grandfather and I used to walk Clark around the neighborhood together before he passed." He says with a bittersweet smile. "He and I became really good buddies. You know, your grand-pop used to speak to me all the time about you."

"Really?" I ask, a bit puzzled that he would have such a good friend that I didn't know about. Then again, I can't really say I knew that many of my grand-pop's friends. I knew he took Clark out for walks a lot, but I just assumed he was by himself.

"It's so nice to finally meet you." he says, "You can call me Manny, I do some of the gardening over at the church."

Still a bit shocked and at a loss for words, I reach out to shake his hand without thinking.

"Oh, sir, I'm so sorry! I didn't mean to." I say, snapping my hand back like I had just touched a hot stove. "I completely forgot. We're supposed to keep 6 feet away from people, especially with…"

I pause for a second, not sure I want to finish the sentence. The old man looks at me and chuckles.

"Especially with us old guys?" He laughs.

This weird sensation runs through my body and I can't quite figure it out. I've been praying recently that I had one more chance to talk to my grand-pop, and in some weird way I feel connected to him just looking at Manny. It's hard to describe, but whatever I'm feeling, I'm strangely not in a rush to get out of this conversation like I typically would be.

"How you doing with everything?" he asks me.

"It's been pretty tough," I say, determined to keep my composure. "With my grand-pop passing, it feels like I lost a huge part of me. Ever since I was little, we did everything together: he took me to school, sports practices, friends' houses, out to eat, on hikes, and to church. So everything feels kind of different."

"I'm so sorry for your loss," Manny says, and I can tell that he means it.

"Thanks," I say. "My parents use to work all the time, before they got laid off due to the Coronavirus. So all of that is different now, too. It's kind of hard being stuck in the house with them because all they want to do is watch the news, worry, and complain.

* * *

"It's a tough season for a lot of people right now," Manny says. "I'm sure they're just doing the best that they can."

"Yeah, I guess," I say, trying not to get choked up. I look down to compose myself, and instinctively grab a hold of the chain with the cross around my neck. "I just need to get out of the house sometimes, you know? So Clark and I go on walks as much as possible, but we usually walk the other way toward the pond, so that's probably why I haven't seen you."

"Probably so." Manny says. "That's a beautiful chain, by the way! Where'd you get it?"

"Grand-pop gave it to me," I say, looking up at Manny. "Just was thinking about him, that's all."

"That's awesome. When did he give it to you?"

"About a year ago, I guess," I say, trying to remember exactly when it was. "I had been asking him some questions about God and faith and stuff, and one day he got me this chain as a surprise and told me Jesus loves me."

"That sounds like your grand-pop," Manny smiles.

"Yeah," I say. "We actually talked a lot about faith. I kind of wish we still could…I still have a lot of questions. In fact, one of our last conversations was a really good one and I couldn't wait to finish it with him. It just stinks that I can't do that now."

I pause for a second and wonder why I'm suddenly spilling my guts to this guy I just met. Maybe because he just helped save my dog's life? Maybe because he knew my grand-pop? Maybe because he looks really old and I just feel sorry for him? I don't know, to be honest.

"Again, I'm so sorry for your loss," Manny says, his big blue eyes glistening in the sun. "He and I had similar conversations, too. I knew him for many years, and I always enjoyed our time together."

"So you guys would talk about deep stuff like faith and God and all of that?" I ask, not totally sure why I'm so interested in keeping the conversation going. I know this guy is not my grand-pop, but for some reason talking to him is making me feel connected to my grand-pop in a way that I haven't felt since he passed.

"Can I ask you a question first?" Manny says with kindness in his voice.

"Yeah, sure." I say, assuming it's going to be related to my grand-pop or how he passed.

"That cross around your neck," he says, "What does that mean to you?"

Chapter 4 - Become Love

I grab the chain and look down at it, trying to gather my thoughts to come up with a good answer.

"I guess it reminds me to be a good person," I say. "Jesus died to save us from our sins, and when I see it, it reminds me to do good things because I'm a Christian."

"So would you say that's the goal of Christianity?" Manny asks.

"Yeah, I think so," I say, feeling pretty confident that I'm right. "The goal is to be a good person so you can go to heaven to spend eternity with God and Jesus."

"Partially correct," Manny says, his smile widening. "Do you mind if I explain?"

"No, go for it," I say, partly because I'm genuinely curious to hear, and partly because anything sounds better than going back home and doing nothing.

"The goal of Christianity is truly Becoming Love by truly

knowing Him and the love He has for each one of us.[1] Yes, Jesus died on that cross to forgive you from sin[2], but He also was raised from the dead so He could put His Spirit on the inside of you.[3] He is not *only* in us so we can go to heaven someday, He is in us so we can bring heaven to this earth by who He is within us[4]; essentially, to let our light shine, right now where we are.[5] Does that make sense?"

"Yeah, I think so," I say, feeling like I've heard some of these ideas before, just not communicated as clearly as Manny is sharing them with me.

"He wants to spend eternity with us," Manny continues, "He also wants to transform us now.[6] That starts with learning to deny yourself[7] and live through His Spirit within you."

Manny pauses for a second, but I don't say anything in response, hoping he'll finish his thought.

"The question really becomes this," Manny says, "Do you desire to become the person he created you for, the person he paid for with His life? Do you truly desire to Become Love?"

"Absolutely." I say, feeling something stirring inside of me. "I guess I've heard people say that everyone has a purpose before, but I don't know if I've ever really thought of it in that

---

[1] 1 Timothy 1:5
[2] John 3:16
[3] John 14:15-18
[4] Galatians 5:22-23
[5] Matthew 5:14-16
[6] Romans 12:2
[7] Matthew 16:24-25

way. That my purpose here is love. To actually become love. I know Jesus said something about loving your neighbor as yourself, but man, that is tough sometimes."

"Loving your neighbor as yourself is difficult because 'you' are the one trying to do it." Manny says. "You are trying to do this on 'your' own. But, if you begin to understand that it's no longer you who lives, but Jesus' Spirit that lives within you,[8] then being a good person and loving your neighbor will be a result.[9] Doing good works is a result of who He is within you.[10] He put His life on the inside of you, so you could express Him. He wants to change you from the inside out."[11]

As Manny is explaining this it's all making sense in my head, and it's kind of making sense in my heart, too. This idea that I don't have it in me to love as deeply as I'm supposed to, but that God is going to help me do that by his Spirit, is kind of freeing in some weird way.

"You still with me?" Manny asks.

"Yeah, I think so," I say. "God's interested in more than just spending eternity with me. He also wants to help me love people the way I'm supposed to while I'm here on earth?"

"Yes," Manny says, "and the way that's going to happen is that He's going to put his Spirit in you and as you seek Him and draw close to Him you will begin to understand how much He loves you. Only then will you truly learn to love

---

[8] Galatians 2:20
[9] Galatians 5:22-23
[10] 1 Corinthians 15:10
[11] Colossians 3:9-10

yourself, because He is True Love. And only then will you be able to truly love others the way they were meant to be loved - with God's love."

A car drives by us and I wonder if the scene looks weird to them. A high schooler with a dog talking to an eighty year old about God. They probably assume he's my grand-pop. I wish he was.

"It all starts by truly knowing how much He loves you," Manny says, pointing at me. "You can learn to truly Love yourself (because he is True Love). Therefore, when you learn to love yourself through His Love for you, you can truly Love people the way they were meant to be Loved — with God's Love. That's how you can Become Love."

This type of love Manny is describing is the type of love my grand-pop had. It seemed like he could *only* love. I never heard him complain or speak negatively about a person. He was such a kind, loving, and patient man.

That's the kind of person I want to be, but I just didn't think I had it in me. And maybe I was right, maybe I don't have it in me. Maybe that's why I need God. In fact now that I think about it, whenever grand-pop was complimented, he would always say, "To God be the glory." I thought it was just his way of saying 'thanks,' but maybe he was actually acknowledging where the love he had came from.

"What are you thinking right now?" Manny asks, and I realize I had been lost in my thoughts for a few seconds.

"I don't know, it's a lot to think about." I say.

* * *

"Have you ever been to the prayer garden?" Manny asks, pointing across the street to the church.

"I didn't even know there was a prayer garden," I say.

"If you have a couple minutes, let me take you over there," he says. "I want to show you something."

within us,' must be planted, rooted, and grounded in quality soil — and the quality soil is God's Love."[1]

"How do I get that quality soil in me?" I ask. "What if I'm not quality soil?"

"That's exactly where I was going with this," Manny says with a smile. "We become rooted and grounded in God's love by reading His Word - specifically His Love for us and how He sees us —from the perspective of 'THIS IS HOW MUCH GOD LOVES ME and THIS IS HOW GOD SEES ME.'"

"So I become quality soil just by reading the Bible?" I ask. "It's that easy?"

"Absolutely, it's not meant to be hard. As we begin seeing how much He Loves us, we continually thank Him for it,[2] and as a result — our faith begins developing through Love —because faith works by love[3], and His Spirit in you begins to grow."

All this talk about trees causes me to pay special attention to the one right in front of us, here in the middle of the garden. I notice how thick the roots are, the type of soil surrounding it, the width of the trunk, the massive amount of tiny branches it has, and the colors of the leaves that are beginning to come in. Noticing that I'm checking out the leaves, Manny comes closer.

"Ah yes, the fruit," he says. "Now through faith the tree

---

[1] Ephesians 3:17
[2] Colossians 2:6-7
[3] Galatians 5:6

grows and grows until it produces the fruit; in the spiritual sense we grow and grow through faith by His Love[4], until we produce the fruit of the Spirit: love, joy, peace, patience kindness, goodness, faithfulness, gentleness, and self-control; the fruit of the Spirit is the result of His presence within us."[5]

"All this fruit talk is making me hungry," I say.

"Well it's funny you say that," Manny replies. "The thing about an apple tree is that it doesn't eat its own fruit, the apple tree is its own fruit. The apples are a result of who the tree is."

"Alright, you're kind of losing me with that one," I say. "Everybody knows that apple trees don't eat apples. I don't see how that applies to us."

"Well, if the apple tree doesn't eat its own fruit," Manny says, "then who does?"

"We do?" I say, not sure if he was looking for an answer or not.

"Yeah, exactly," Manny laughs. "Animals and people. They come by and get to eat the fruit that the tree produced. And when they take the fruit, the seed comes with it. Just by living — how you talk and act, people will be able to experience Jesus' fruit through you."[6]

"Okay, that makes a little more sense," I say. "The point of

---

[4] Colossians 2:6-7, Galatians 5:6
[5] Galatians 5:22-23
[6] Galatians 5:22-23

this tree idea is that my life is giving off some kind of fruit that other people will experience. So, like, the reason my grand-pop was different was because I was experiencing Jesus through his life? That was his fruit?"

"Absolutely," Manny says. "Because of His relationship with Jesus, your grand-pop became more like Him. It's the same for anyone who becomes rooted and grounded in God's Love. It allows us to live by His Spirit within us, and as a result, we produce His fruit. We are able to produce Heaven on earth by who He is within us."

I look back at the tree and marvel at its beauty, wishing grand-pop was there with me in that moment.

"Sadly, most people grow up in the world's system," Manny says, looking me in the eyes. "They become trees with all sorts of bad fruit on it. People grow up hating, fearing, worrying, stressing, struggling with sexual immorality, and that sort of thing. Some struggle with addiction: whether that's with food, cigarettes, alcohol, drugs, etc. which becomes the fruit that is on their tree."[7]

"You see, at your age, you're trying to figure out who you are, whether you realize it or not. Most kids are a product of how they reacted to what they have been through, but that was never God's intention. At your age if you begin to see who you are from the perspective of how God sees you and how much He loves you, you'll be molded into this tree that produces His Fruit— filled with Love."

"So is that why the world has so much bad stuff in it," I ask,

---

[7] Matthew 12:33

"because of all the bad fruit people are producing?"

"Yeah, that's mostly true," Manny says, "but it's a little more complicated than that." He pauses for a minute, as if he's not sure he wants to explain what he meant.

"Keep going, I'm listening." I say. For all I know, this is the last time I'll ever talk to this guy about God. Might as well hear him out.

"Okay, well if you want to keep talking, let's keep walking," Manny says. "I've gotta get my steps in, and I bet Clark does, too."

PART TWO

ORIGINS

I have a brain like the Bermuda Triangle. Information goes in, never to be found again!

Chapter 6 - Where it all Began

We head out of the garden, around the back end of the church, and through the field as Manny picks the conversation back up.

"Think about the all of the issues and messes we have going on in this world right now. All of the evil, the tons of negativity, and all of the awful, terrible things that are going on around us. People always say — why do bad things happen to good people? Well, where does that originate?"

I keep quiet this time, assuming it's a rhetorical question.

"God didn't make us to be angry, evil, frustrated, jealous, unforgiving, antagonistic, and ticked off. He doesn't want us to constantly be comparing ourselves with others. He didn't desire any of that; He actually made us in His image.[1] We were born with those things because of Adam's separation from God in the Garden of Eden. We are all descendants of Adam until we accept Jesus as Lord and Savior. Then, we are

---

[1] Genesis 1:27

spiritually reborn.[2]

"From the time we can remember, we needed support, value, and attention; and people get crushed in that arena. They either become broken and introverted and insecure, or hard and calloused and a fighter. By a very young age we're nothing more than what we became through how we responded to what we'd been through. And our story has become our identity and not the truth of who we really are in Christ, and why we're really here."

"Sounds depressing," I mutter.

"But it's not," Manny says, "because we can all find our true identity in God. It can only be found in Christ.[3] His Spirit and His Word will reveal this to you.[4] If He is Love, then you are Love, because of His Spirit within you.[5] We were created to believe. We were created to trust. We were created to be the blessing and the Good News on this earth. We were called to walk in His image. This is who we truly are. When we accept Jesus Christ as Lord and Savior, we are taken out of Adam's genes and put into Christ[6] — remember that new seed was planted right here."

The old man puts his finger on the right at my heart as he says this last line, and the weight of it sinks in, in a good way.

"This is where we were originally supposed to be," he

---

[2] 1 Corinthians 5:17-21
[3] Galatians 2:20
[4] 1 Corinthians 2:10-16, John 14:26
[5] 1 John 4:15-16
[6] 2 Corinthians 5:17, Romans 5:15-19

continues. "the key is having the Life of Christ come alive on the inside of you.[7] As this happens, you transform into His image and become all that He originally called you to be[8] — in this example, like the tree. We are all in need of a Savior. We all need saving.[9] Understanding the history and why we need saving can be very powerful."

I look down at Clark and wonder if he has any idea of just how fascinating these ideas are, and almost laugh out loud at the thought of a dog understanding a conversation about God.

"Okay, so why do we need saving in the first place?" I ask, partly because I want to know and partly to show that I've been paying attention.

"You have to go all the way back to the Garden of Eden with Adam and Eve." Manny says. "That's where our need of saving comes from. With the act of eating the apple, Adam turned over everything God had given him to Satan.[10] God had given Adam complete dominion and authority over this earth. God loved Adam and Eve so much that he gave Adam and Eve Himself. He literally empowered them with Himself. So when Adam and Eve committed high treason by eating the apple, they literally took everything God had given to them and gave it to Satan; including dominion and authority over this earth.[11] So when that happened, God had a serious problem ahead of Him. God could not legally get back into

---

[7] Romans 8:10-11
[8] Colossians 3:9-10, Romans 12:2
[9] Romans 3:23
[10] Luke 4:5-7
[11] Luke 4:5-7

this earth to do His Will, to do what He desired until He could reconcile what had happened with Adam and Eve in the Garden."[12]

"Yeah, but here's something I've never understood," I say, interjecting. "If God had the power to create the earth, why couldn't he just go back into his creation and correct what happened? Why couldn't He intervene if things started to get screwed up?"

"God is a sovereign God, but He has sovereignly said He is not going to break His word." Manny says. "He swore by Himself that He would never lie.[13] So in other words, He swore that He would never break his word. He gave dominion and authority over to Adam and Eve, and they turned over all authority God had given them over to Satan. God was not surprised by any this, but he needed to reverse what happened."

"Let me guess," I say, "that has to do with this cross around my neck?"

"Essentially, yes," Manny says, "Hang on a sec, we'll get there."

---

[12] Genesis 22:15-18
[13] Titus 1:2

Chapter 7 - Keys to the House

"So you understand why God couldn't go back on His word?" Manny asks.

"Yeah, I think so," I say.

"Think of it this way," Manny says, pointing to the country style house with a wrap around porch and a stone chimney next to the church. "Let's pretend that this house is my house. If I gave you my word and said you can have my house, then it's your house, right?"

I look up at him not sure if it's a trick question or not.

"No seriously," he says, slowly pulling his keys out of his pocket and dropping them in my hand. "If I gave you the keys and signed over the deed so that this was your house, it would be your house, right?"

"Yeah," I say, going along with him.

"So then, if some scammer came along and deceived you into giving away all of the rights to the house so that he owned it, it would be his house, right?"

***

"Yup."

"At that point can I legally do anything to get the house back from the scammer?"

"Probably not," I say, "because when you gave me the rights, you gave up your rights."

"That's right, and that's a lot of rights" Manny says, laughing at his own joke. "The only way I could get back the rights to the house would be to get them from the scammer. I'd need to find a way to get them from him or someone who lived in his house."

"Woah," I reply, "yeah I get that. I never thought of it like that. Keys to the house, I like that. Although if I'm honest, it still doesn't make complete sense why God let that happen in the first place."

"He didn't let it happen," Manny responds. "He loved people so much that He 'blessed' them. He created a world for them to enjoy and gave them complete dominion and authority. Man was just deceived."

"I guess I get that," I say, still processing the idea.

"I like that you're not afraid to ask those big, tough questions," Manny says. "Don't let them hold you back. Remember, it's all about child-like faith."

I nod my head in agreement, remembering that my grand-pop used to use that phrase when I was little. "Never lose this faith you have, you just believe." He used to say. I never fully understood what he meant then, but I think I'm starting to get it now.

"So Jesus came back to grab the keys to the house from Satan?" I ask, trying to guess where he was going next.

"Now don't skip ahead," he says, pulling a treat out of his pocket and giving it to Clark, "there's a lot more to this story."

Clark devours the treat while Manny pats his back, and then we start moving again. We make our way through the field away from the church as he continues.

"After sometime, there came a pivotal moment in our history. In the time of Noah, the world was so bad and corrupted with evil that God grieved in His heart that He created man. The wickedness of the people was so great that the thoughts and intents of their hearts were only evil, continually.[1]

"Wait, why were people so jacked up right away?" I interrupt him. "Why so much bad fruit?"

"Due to the disconnect from God because of Adam and Even in the garden," Manny says, "over those hundreds of years people's hearts grew colder and harder and more evil. Except for Noah, that is. Noah found grace in the eyes of the Lord, and he and his family were the only people on earth not corrupted by evil."[2] There's a little more to the story than that, but the point is, things were bad."

* * *

---

[1] Genesis 6:5-6
[2] Genesis 6

"God warned Noah that a flood was coming and instructed him on how to build the ark. By faith, Noah was moved by Godly fear (awe and respect for God) and he followed God's detailed plan for the ark. As a result, he became the heir of righteousness (right standing relationship with God) — because of His faith.

"Now, without understanding the full extent of what happened in the flood, you may think God killed innocent people. In reality, the ones who died in the flood were all of an evil, corrupted, and demonic generation."[3]

"I was kind of wondering about that," I said. "Seems like a harsh move by God to just wipe everyone out."

"Well, God so loved mankind that He saved them through Noah and his family. It wasn't that Noah's family was perfect; this wasn't about God saving them because of anything they did. But the Bible says that Noah found grace in God's eyes, so He made a covenant with Noah that He would never destroy the earth like He did with the flood. He did this despite knowing that the imagination of a man's heart is evil from his youth — due to the fall in the garden."

"So you're saying that God didn't expect Noah to repopulate the world with a bunch of people who would never do anything wrong?" I ask.

"No," Manny chuckled, "I guess you could say He's a lot smarter than that."

---

[3] Genesis 6:12

Chapter 8 - Abraham and Isaac

We let a few walkers with dogs on the church's driveway walk by us without causing too much commotion with Clark, then we walk over to a spot in the field where Manny had left a bottle from earlier.

"Want me to get you one of these?" He asks, holding up his water bottle. "At my age I need to stay hydrated."

"Nah, I'm good thanks," I say. "But I gotta say, for as smart as God is, it sort of sounds like He's playing catch up this whole time."

"What do you mean by that?" Manny asks, taking a sip of his water.

"I don't know," I say, "God creates man and man screws up in the garden, gives away the keys to the house, and then gets so evil that He wipes out everyone but one family. Hard not to think that it was all a big mistake at that point."

"Once again," Manny says, "this is where we get into the brilliance of God. You see, God is omniscient. He knows the end from the beginning.[1] He still knew what was going to happen. Right from the point that Adam did what he did, God had already developed a plan to get His Son into this earth."

As he says this, my hand goes up to the cross on my neck. Manny is not even done sharing all of this with me and the chain already has more meaning to me than it ever had before.

"God still needed to find a man that was willing to come into covenant with Him to perform the ultimate sacrifice," Manny continues, "A man that would enable God to get back into this earth. And He found it in a man named Abraham.[2] Abraham was not only willing to listen to God and believe Him, he would come into covenant with Him.[3] He actually found a man that was willing to sacrifice his true, only begotten son based on what God had told him to do when his faith in God was put to the test."[4]

"I think I may have heard this story before," I say.

"You probably have," Manny says. "Abraham was an old man, 100 years of age and his wife, Sarah, was 90 years old and had been barren without children. After the Lord came to Abraham and told him they would conceive a child a year from that day and that he would be the father of many nations Abraham believed Him full-heartedly. So when God asked Abraham to offer his only true begotten son, Isaac, as a

---

[1] Revelation 1:8
[2] Genesis 12:1-4
[3] Genesis 17
[4] Genesis 22:9-12

sacrifice,[5] you can only imagine how hard that would be for a person to do."

"Yeah, and confusing," I add.

"Exactly," Manny says, "but Abraham trusted God. And when his faith was tested to the point where he was actually willing to sacrifice his only true begotten son Isaac, the Angel of the Lord stopped Abraham and prevented him from doing it.[6] This was the ultimate covenant act that opened the door for God to be able to get back into this earth to get His Son Jesus on earth. Abraham's act of faith and trust in God showed why God had chosen him to be the one to start the chain of bringing Jesus into this earth."[7]

"I can't imagine my dad being willing to offer me up like that," I say. "Abraham must have trusted God on a whole different level. It almost doesn't seem right."

"Exactly, in the natural that seems so difficult. But Abraham trusted God, and his trust was rewarded. The rest of the stories in the Old Testament are so powerful, especially if you can learn to see Jesus in every book, chapter, verse, and word. But again the point of this conversation isn't to dive into the history of the Old Testament. I just wanted to make sure you were up to date with the significance of getting Jesus into this earth and a brief summary of how that process went down to give you a better understanding of that cross you're wearing."

* * *

---

[5] Genesis 22:1-2
[6] Genesis 22:11-12
[7] Genesis 22:15-18

"Have you ever thought about teaching?" I say, only half-joking.

"I've done a little teaching in my day," he smiles.

"Honestly, some of the history stuff is a little confusing," I say, "but I keep thinking about how my purpose here is to Become Love and bear good fruit for other people. It seems so simple, in a good way."

"That makes me happy to hear," Manny says. "It's meant to be simple. Now let me get into Jesus."

PART THREE

THE CROSS

Chapter 9 - Jesus, an Act of Love

We make our way toward the end of the long church field and driveway when Manny turns around, fixing his eyes on the cross above the church. I stop with him and Clark lays down to catch his breath.

"Due to the covenant between Abraham and God," Manny starts, "God was legally able to get Jesus into this earth. In the Old Testament, year after year, sacrifices of unblemished animals were required to pardon people of their sins. Because it was required year after year, the sacrifices were not perfect.[1] A perfect sacrifice would be of One who did not commit one sin, that was fully pure, and it would require no other further sacrifices.[2]

"God sent His only begotten Son into this world to save it.[3] Jesus was fully God and fully man.[4] He is a man that is in

---

[1] Hebrews 10:1-4
[2] Hebrews 10:10, Hebrews 10:16-18
[3] John 3:16-17
[4] John 1:14

perfect relationship with God.[5] Jesus' ministry lasted roughly 3 years: spreading the gospel, teaching people, healing the sick, casting out demons, and performing miracles. Jesus showed us perfectly what a perfect relationship with the Father looks like.[6]

"So wait, Jesus was God, but he wasn't like an angel or something?" I ask. "You're saying he was actually human, too."

"That's right," Manny says. "He was born of a woman, and he grew up from an infant to a child to a man just like us. And yet He was also God as well."

"That's hard to wrap my head around," I say.

"That's fine," Manny says. "I like that you're willing to admit that."

"So Jesus is God, and yet He lets the government kill him?"

"At the end of His ministry on earth, Jesus was condemned to death by Pontius Pilate due to the Jewish leaders who believed Jesus was a blasphemer.[7] After being brutally beaten and maliciously whipped,[8] He had a crown of thorns put on His head[9] before He was made to carry His cross. To keep this PG-13, He was so brutally beaten and whipped you could not make out who He was — no man ever looked the way He

---

[5] John 14:9
[6] John 5:19
[7] Mark 14:61-65
[8] John 19:1
[9] John 19:2

did.[10] Can you imagine seeing someone beaten so bad that you couldn't distinguish who He was?"

I shake my head no, but don't say anything so Manny will keep going with the story.

"Despite having to carry His cross to Calvary and despite being beaten and whipped along the way, Jesus still only had Love in His heart. In His entire lifetime, Jesus never committed one sin, never spoke one lie,[11] always loved; and yet He was still tortured and beaten. Even in the midst of being mocked and tortured, Jesus prayed for everyone as He was on the cross saying, 'Father, forgive them. For they know not what they do.'[12]

"When He reaches Calvary, the Roman soldiers crucified Him; they hammered giant nails into both of His hands and feet.[13] As they put him up on the cross, the Jewish leaders mocked him saying, 'He saved others; Himself He cannot save. Let the Christ, the King of Israel, descend now from the cross, that we may see and believe.'[14]

"Man, just hearing that makes me wish he did save himself." I say. "How great would it have been if he just pulled himself off the cross and showed them who He really was."

"What's interesting is, He couldn't do that." Manny says. "He

---

[10] Isaiah 52:14
[11] 1 Peter 2:22
[12] Luke 23:34
[13] Mark 15:24-26
[14] Mark 15:31

physically couldn't, because Love doesn't seek its own; love isn't selfish.[15] He was up on the cross and the only thing on His mind was to fulfill the will of the Father.[16] And what is the will of the Father?"

Manny pauses before answering his own question. "For God so loved the world that He gave His only begotten Son, that whoever believes in Him should not perish but have everlasting life."

"John 3:16, right?" I say.

"That's right" Manny says. "Love gives. And God GAVE His only begotten Son so that we could be saved; connected back to Him; brought back in as His sons and daughters.[17] He purchased us with the blood of Jesus."[18]

"What's the significance of the cross?" I ask, grabbing the one around my neck. "Why the cross?"

"For it is said, He who hangs on a tree (the cross) is cursed."[19] Manny says. "That's one of the many ways Jesus fulfilled all that was written in the Old Testament. He became a curse for us, so that we could inherit the blessing, God's Grace (His Spirit within us). He became a curse for us, so we didn't have to be,[20] and because He was the only one ever to live without

---

[15] 1 Corinthians 13:5
[16] Luke 22:42
[17] Ephesians 1:5, Galatians 3:26
[18] Ephesians 1:7, Galatians 3:13-15
[19] Deuteronomy 21:23
[20] Galatians 3:13-14

sin, death had no power over Him.[21] When He was on the cross, He gave up His Spirit;[22] He couldn't die, even from the torture He was put through.

"We were so in debt with sin, that God gave His Son as a perfect, pure, holy, and blameless sacrifice once and for all[23] so that when we believe and accept Him as Lord and Savior, He puts His Spirit in our hearts,[24] which then becomes our new identity.[25] God bought us back from sin and death,[26] and blessed us with his grace on top of it.

Clark stands up, and starts licking my hand. I think he's ready to get going again, but I'm happy to stand here and listen to Manny explain this stuff to me.

"You see," Manny says, "God sees you as holy and blameless. He has forgiven you of all sin because of the blood of Jesus.[27] He has paid for your sins and has connected you back to the father. By the stripes (whippings) on His back, you are healed.[28] He was wounded for our transgressions and bruised for our sin.[29] He bore all of the world's sin, condemnation, sickness, death, etc on Himself at the cross and defeated Satan, sin, and death forever.[30] He made it easy

---

[21] Romans 6:9, Romans 6:23
[22] John 19:30
[23] Hebrews 10:14-18
[24] Ephesians 1:13-14
[25] 2 Corinthians 5:17
[26] Romans 8:2
[27] Ephesians 1:4-7
[28] 1 Peter 2:24
[29] Isaiah 53:4-5
[30] 1 Corinthians 15:55-57

on us, He did all of the hard work. He went through all of that, so we could be with Him now and forever in heaven; Knowing Him is eternal life;[31] If we believe in Him.[32]

"We are more than conquerers through Him.[33] We are transformed from glory to glory in His image.[34] We are accepted in God's family as His children.[35] We are saved because of Jesus. You see, when He was getting whipped beyond comprehension, beaten, tortured, and nailed to the cross, He had love on His mind. He loved us so much and was so committed to do God's Will, there was no turning back.

"Through Jesus, we can reign in this life as conquerors — if we begin to see ourselves as God sees us and what we have because of Jesus.[36] Like He said as His last words, 'It Is Finished.'[37] We have been given His grace and been made righteous (made right with God or seen as right in his eyes) because of what Jesus did for us;[38] because of His Love for us; because of the finished work of the cross. We must develop our faith in God's love for us and the finished work of the cross."

We both stand there in silence for a few minutes, letting Manny's words hang in the air.

---

[31] John 17:3
[32] John 3:16-17
[33] Romans 8:37
[34] 2 Corinthians 3:18
[35] 1 John 3:1-2
[36] Romans 5:17
[37] John 19:30
[38] Romans 5:16-17

* * *

"Seems like Clark is ready to get moving again," Manny says.

"He'll be fine for another few minutes," I say, looking over at Manny, who isn't looking at me, but is still looking up at the cross. As he does, a single tear runs down his cheek and falls to the ground.

Chapter 10 - The Power of His Victory

I stand there for a moment in silence, still holding tight to the cross that's on my neck. I think about asking Manny if he's okay, but I can tell he is. It seems like a tear of joy or gratefulness, not sadness.

"So, that's the gospel," Manny finally says. "That's the good news. Through the Life of His Son, God showed us and taught us what a world would look like if we were truly in right relationship with Him. Jesus literally produced Heaven on Earth."

"It doesn't seem like heaven down here most of the time," I say.

"I know," Manny says. "Jesus was the final, pure, and blameless sacrifice that abolished sin and death and connected us back to the Father. Through Jesus' Life, death, and resurrection, God and Jesus defeated sin and death forever. But not everyone chooses to believe that and to walk in the power of His Spirit.

"When Jesus ascended into Heaven, God blessed us all with

the Gift of His Spirit (His Grace — the unmerited gift and blessing). Although, we were born into sin through Adam, we have the choice to accept Jesus as our personal Lord and Savior. As a result, God's Spirit will literally live and dwell on the inside of us if we put our faith in Him.

"Not only were our slates wiped completely clean by the blood of Jesus, we were literally made pure and blameless in the eyes of God. God sees us through the lens of the Blood of Jesus. Through Jesus, we are saved and have been given the gift of and been made righteous. We were removed from the sin foundation and placed in the righteous foundation."[1]

"This might be a dumb question," I say, interrupting him, "but what does 'righteous' mean? I've heard that word so many times, but I don't think I really know what it means."

"That's not a dumb question at all," Manny smiles. "Not many people understand righteousness. Let me see if I can explain this as simply as possible."

"Righteousness, simply in its purest form, is a right standing relationship with God. It means you are seen as right in the eyes of God.[2] Righteous would be the opposite of sin and evil."

"In the Old Testament, under the Law and Commandments, God DEMANDED righteousness from the people.[3] But it was impossible for them to achieve it because once a person sins

---

[1] 2 Corinthians 5:21
[2] Romans 3:22-24, 2 Corinthians 5:21
[3] Romans 8:3-4, Galatians 3:10-14

one time, He is guilty of the entire law.[4] Even if it's just the smallest sin, it's still sin. Being righteous is being holy, without blame, in a right standing relationship with God."[5]

"That's kind of harsh, isn't it?" I say. "You sin one time and it makes you guilty of everything?"

"Let's take this water bottle for example," Manny says, holding it up to eye level. "Let's say I drop a couple drops of gasoline in it. Would it be drinkable?"

"Is it regular or unleaded?" I joke, which gets Manny to laugh.

"How about one drop of each," he chuckles. "Just two drops of fuel, and that's it. Would you drink it?"

"No, wouldn't touch it." I say.

"Exactly," he says. "Same with sin. Once you sin, the water (you) becomes contaminated, and no longer pure. Although, in the New Testament, under grace (His Spirit within you), righteousness is SUPPLIED/GIVEN to you because of Jesus' sacrifice."[6]

He holds the water bottle up again. "So the once contaminated bottle of water is now purified in God's eyes because of Jesus."

"Okay, I think I get that," I say.

---

[4] James 2:10
[5] 2 Corinthians 5:21
[6] Romans 3:21-24

* * *

"When Christ's Spirit is in you, God sees you as a righteous, new creation.[7] He doesn't see you as the old sinner anymore. Your old spirit has passed away, behold, God sees you as a brand new spirit, His Spirit within you.[8] Now, you've been made pure and blameless by the blood of Jesus."[9]

"You see, we can find rest in His Spirit because we don't have to work for righteousness (seen as right in God's eyes) anymore and once you begin to see yourself how God sees you,[10] you'll begin to produce the fruit of righteousness as a result.[11] Most people think they have to work for their salvation.[12] Simply put, that's wrong."

"It's not always easy to do the right thing, though," I say.

"No, it's definitely not," Manny says, "though God's Spirit will help you with that. But remember, your salvation and the righteousness God sees in you has nothing to do with what you did. It has to do with what Jesus did for you."

"In the Amplified Bible, The Bible that helps interpret the meaning of words translated from the old Hebrew, Aramaic, and Greek languages, it depicts this so well in Ephesians 2:8-9. It says:

"For it is by grace [God's remarkable compassion and favor

---

[7] Romans 3:25-26, 2 Corinthians 5:21
[8] 2 Corinthians 5:17-21
[9] Ephesians 1:4-7
[10] Hebrews 4:1-10
[11] Philippians 1:9-11, Galatians 5:22-23
[12] Ephesians 2:2, Romans 10:8-10, John 3:16-21

drawing you to Christ] that you have been saved [actually delivered from judgment and given eternal life] through faith. And this [salvation] is not of yourselves [not through your own effort], but it is the [undeserved, gracious] gift of God; not as a result of [your] works [nor your attempts to keep the Law], so that no one will [be able to] boast or take credit in any way [for his salvation]."

"Okay, wow," I say. "So all of this righteousness and salvation has nothing to do with what I do, whether it's a bunch of good stuff or a bunch of bad stuff?"

"You can't earn it, no," Manny says. "But at the same time, it doesn't give you permission to go do whatever you want and be reckless. But what it does do, is give us the ability to rest and start our journey from where Jesus finished."

"So the fruit I'm producing is not what determines my salvation?" I ask.

"Right," Manny says. "Your salvation is about your faith and believing in Jesus."

"But the fruit is important," I say, "because it's how other people can experience God and see how good He is."

"That's exactly right," Manny says, stooping down to give Clark another treat. "I think Clark here has had enough rest at this point. Let's get moving again."

Chapter 11 - The Direct Connection

"Yeah, we should probably start making our way back home soon," I say. " I guess I gotta go home at some point."

Home. It's crazy how I hadn't really thought about it since Manny and I started talking. All the bad news and bickering and talk of viruses and quarantine. It felt great to be talking about good news instead of bad, and everything Manny had shared with me really did seem like good news. As I thought about it, I felt joy stir inside of me that I hadn't felt in a while.

"Hey, I see a smile breaking out on your face," Manny says to me.

"I guess I was just thinking about how my grand-pop used to call all of this stuff about Jesus, the 'Good News,' and now I get it."

"It is definitely good news," Manny says, "and we just covered a bunch of stuff. Do you have any questions?"

"I'm sure I will as I process it all," I say, "but nothing comes to mind at the moment."

* * *

"To sum it up again," Manny says, "Jesus redeemed the world from sin and death and gave us a path back to God. And through Jesus, God can forgive our sins and our pasts, wiping us completely clean and allowing us to move forward becoming rooted and grounded in His Love, by giving us HIS SPIRIT and His Word."

"We no longer have to look back and live in guilt and condemnation about our past.[1] All we have to do is repent of our sins with a sincere heart, believe in what Jesus did, and through the empowerment of the Holy Spirit in us completely turn away from sin and focus on God's Light.[2]

"It sounds too easy to get a clean slate when you put it that way," I say.

"Who said it had to be hard?" Manny responds. "Through Jesus' life, death, and resurrection, we were given Jesus' same Spirit that lives and dwells on the inside of us; a true spiritual rebirth. As a result, we now have a direct connection with God, that literally lives in our hearts. The Holy Spirit is our Helper, Comforter, Advocate, Intercessor, Counselor, Strengthener, Standby;[3] He is our own personal GPS through life, that if we learn to follow Him we will be living a life led by God.

"Our own GPS," I say, nodding my head. "I like that."

"And if that still isn't enough," Manny says, "God literally accepts and welcomes us into His family as His Children and

---

[1] Romans 8:1-2
[2] 1 John 1:6-9, Acts 3:19
[3] John 14:26

has made us joint heirs with Jesus Christ.[4]

"All this sounds a little too good to be true," I say, with a little bit of skepticism. "You're saying that God wants to forgive us for the mistakes we've made, give us His Spirit to help us live, and welcome us into His family, whatever that means. I guess it's a pretty nice version of God if it's true."

"Well, it is," Manny smiles. "God loves us so much. We were once lost, but now we are found. He's redeemed us from the world of sin and death, He has forgiven and delivered us from our sin, He shows us mercy, He purified us from our past sin, He gave us His Spirit to guide and teach us through Life, and He calls us His children — all by the sacrifice of His Son, Jesus. He is our Healer, our Comforter, our loving God.

Manny pauses for a second and then points to my chain, "THAT IS THE FINISHED WORK OF THE CROSS."

I look up at him and our eyes meet. Wiping his eyes, he smiles at me and nods his head. Quite frankly, I'm at a loss for words, but I try to find some.

"Sir, that was amazing." I say. "I've never heard someone speak with such passion and love before. That was so simple and easy to follow as well."

"Glad to hear," he smiles. "Let's keep on. Don't want you to be late for dinner."

---

[4] Galatians 4:6-7

Chapter 12 - The Lost Sheep

We make our way down the driveway and onto the street. Clark is trotting along, happy as can be to be moving again. I can't believe how close he was to getting hit by that truck not too long ago. I still don't understand where Manny came from and how the two of them didn't get run over.

We walk quietly for a few moments, and suddenly a thought occurs to me.

"I actually do have a question now that I think about it," I say. "How does God feel about the people that have done really bad things? I know I struggle with the idea of forgiving someone if they killed someone, or did something terrible like that."

Manny takes a sips of water and asks, "Have you ever heard of the story of the Lost Sheep?"

"Maybe," I say, "but refresh my memory."

"Well, Jesus was constantly ridiculed by the Pharisees because he welcomed sinners," Manny says. "So Jesus asks them all if they all had 100 sheep and lost one of them, would they not leave the 99 to go find the one?

"He ends the question with the statement, '...There will be more joy in heaven over one sinner who repents than over 99 righteous people who have no need of repentance'[1]."

"Jesus was making it pretty clear," Manny says, "He came for the sinners. He came as the bridge between God and man. Jesus is the way for us to bridge the gap over sin. He not only came as our teacher, he gave us the gift of His Spirit to help us navigate through life — to continue living a life led by God. Without the Spirit, it is impossible to habitually live Christ-like, without sin.[2]

"So you're saying if I try to produce good fruit on my own without God, I'll never do it?" I ask.

"God says in His word that all men have sinned and have fallen short of the glory of God.[3] Furthermore, the man who keeps the whole law but falls short of one point, is accountable for all.[4] Does that make sense? We all fall short of the glory of God. It doesn't matter if we break all of the laws or just one. As a result, this is why it was necessary for Jesus to come to not only set the example and be relatable to humans because He is God in human form, but also so the gift of His Spirit within each one of us can guide us and lead us to sin no more.

"But don't think the law doesn't matter anymore," Manny

---

[1] Luke 15:1-7
[2] Galatians 5:16-17
[3] Romans 3:23
[4] James 2:10

continued. "The 10 commandments are still beautiful and a wonderful guideline. But through His Spirit within us, we uphold the law.[5] Jesus fulfilled the law.[6] And if we learn to live through His Spirit within us, we as well will not be under law, but under grace, because His Spirit never broke the law.[7] Remember, we have His exact same Spirit in our hearts.[8] Also, you must keep in mind, it is no longer you doing the works, it is Him within you doing the works."[9]

"I get all that and it sounds great," I say, interrupting him before he gets any further, "but think about what you're saying. You're telling me that the guy that kills someone is at the same level as the guy who disobeys his parents?! That's crazy!"

"It is not our place to be the judge." Manny responds, calmly. "If we're judging each other, we are putting ourselves as superior to them. If that's the case, then we are falling under pride — which is not a fruit of the Spirit, but of the flesh (sinful nature).[10] Instead Jesus teaches us to pray for our enemies, not judge them.[11] If you remember, before Jesus died on the cross, he asked God to forgive the Jews and the Romans, because the people did not know what they were doing.[12] Jesus asked His Father in Heaven to forgive the

---

[5] Romans 3:31, Romans 8:3-4, Galatians 5:22-23
[6] Matthew 5:17-20
[7] Romans 6:14
[8] 2 Corinthians 1:22
[9] Philippians 2:13, 1 Corinthians 15:10
[10] 1 John 2:16
[11] Matthew 5:45-47
[12] Luke 23:34

people that maliciously tortured and killed him before he died.

"Isn't true love thinking of others more highly than yourself?[13] The Bible doesn't say there are exceptions to love. Imagine if the world would stop ridiculing and pointing the finger at each other, but would simply love their neighbor and pray for people that are doing wrong things. Jesus says love and pray for your enemies.

"I don't really have any enemies," I say. "But if I did, I'm not sure I would love them."

"It's a hard command," Manny says, "but it's what Jesus did. Now, as for the murderer. If someone committed murder, they are not truly living through His Spirit within them, because Jesus would never commit murder.[14] So if they are not being led by Him, who are they be misled by? The enemy comes to steal, kill, and destroy.[15] The problem is, the person who committed murder is being "blindfolded" by Satan and they can no longer see the Truth, the Light, and the Way."

"Now if that very same individual that committed murder, begins to see the Truth, the True Love of God, and sincerely repents of his sins to God and begs God to forgive him of his sins; He wants to be a changed man and from that day forward lives His life for God, God will truly accept Him and give that man His Grace. His past will be completely

---

[13] Philippians 2:3, 1 Corinthians 13:4-8
[14] Galatians 5:22-23
[15] John 10:10

forgotten[16] and he will be seen by God as a new creation.[17]

"I guess I like that idea," I say. "I mean, the idea of a God who is willing to forgive someone who truly feels bad about what they did and wants to change. It would stink if God was like, 'sorry, you blew your chance and I'm done with you'."

"And remember," Manny says, "it's not just that He is willing to forgive, but that He takes great joy in it, right? So much so that Jesus said there will be more joy in heaven for one sinner who repents, over 99 righteous people who are in no need of repentance.[18]

"That is pretty amazing," I say, feeling my heart soften even as the words come out.

---

[16] Hebrews 8:12
[17] 2 Corinthians 5:17
[18] Luke 15:7

Chapter 13 - *You are The ONE*

"Going back to the murderer, though," I say, "I just never thought of it as being judgmental when I thought what they did was wrong."

"Well, obviously what they did was very wrong," Manny says, "but this is about how we view ourselves compared to others and how God views us. God warns us to be careful of judging one another, because if you judge another, you are regarding yourself as higher or better. And if that's the case, you fall more under pride than Love. Those who humble themselves will be exalted and those who exalt themselves will be humbled.[1] In humility, value others above yourself. Remember, Love is not proud.[2]

"The world would be a much better place if people reacted to people who committed murder and other injustices with Love by simply praying for them and showing them the Light. When we ridicule others and judge them, we are not truly Loving them — stemming from God's Love for each one

---

[1] Matthew 23:12
[2] 1 Corinthians 13:4

of us. As a result, we fall back right into the deception and trap of satan."

"You're not talking about the police or judges, right?" I say.

"No, I'm not talking about the legal system and the punishment for breaking laws our government has set up," Manny clarifies. "When done well, those things are a benefit to society and God tells us to honor them. I'm talking about how, as fellow humans, we view others and love others."

"Gotcha."

"If we are not Loving others with the Love stemming from God's Love for us but judging others because they committed a sin that in our opinion is worse then we have done, who are we following after? We are actually throwing gasoline on the flame, and that flame is not the Holy Spirit. We are actually throwing darkness upon darkness — putting a black marker on top of a black marker."

"It's almost depressing when you think about it," I say, lowering my head and patting Clark's head. "I can see how this world has fallen into a vicious cycle. Someone does something wrong and then people jump on their throat. It's cut throat and not led by Love."

"Son, remember, there is no need to feel guilt from this." Manny says. "There is no guilt and condemnation in Christ Jesus.[3] He has already forgiven us of our sins — past, present, and future.[4] Allowing God to convict us is fine, because that's

---

[3] Romans 8:1
[4] Hebrews 10:16-17, Ephesians 1:3-14

how He shows us the areas where we need to change to live more like Him. Even when we slip up, He is right there with open arms waiting for us to come back to Him.

"Since we have Him in our hearts, He makes our conscience clear. Our consciences will allow us to feel when we have been led astray. As a result, we will be able to come straight back to Him much quicker than we would have if we weren't led by Him. Remember, the aim of our instruction is Love, which stems from a pure heart, a good clear conscience and a sincere faith.[5]

"Although we are blessed to have Jesus' Spirit in our hearts and we were given the mind of Christ,[6] we cannot stop there. We must continue to be committed to developing a relationship with Him — remember, a relationship is a two-way street. As we continue to know Him more and develop a closer relationship with Him, our minds become renewed and as a result will not be transformed by this world.[7] The transformation comes from growing and developing your relationship with Jesus and His Spirit within you.[8]

"This is pretty heavy stuff," I say. "But in a good, way, I guess."

"It is a very difficult topic to truly understand." Manny sighs. "The depth of God's love is so deep, its hard to imagine that someone commits a murder and can be still loved by God. We have all committed sin and we all don't deserve His Grace,

---

[5] 1 Timothy 1:5
[6] 1 Corinthians 2:16
[7] Romans 12:2
[8] Colossians 3:9-10, 2 Corinthians 3:18

but he Loves us so much that He gave it to us anyway.

"I guess I like the thought that nothing I can do can put me beyond the reach of God's love." I say.

"That's a great way to put it," Manny says. "And your job is to truly Love others, no matter what they do. If someone hurts you, still Love. Hurt for them that they don't see the Light. Be their Light. If you truly Love them and He is living through you, you may be the Light they need to finally see the Truth. Instead of ridiculing others, pray for them. Become forgiveness. Become Merciful. Because He is Forgiveness, He is Merciful."

"You're talking about that good fruit again."

"Exactly. And remember, we were all born into sin, but through Him we are saved and are able to produce good fruit. No matter what type of sin you have committed, YOU ARE THE ONE sheep that God misses and wants to bring back. He Loves each one of us like that ONE sheep. He does not hate you, because Love is not Hate. And we must remember, God is Love.

"God will accept you with open arms and will be filled with Joy when you return to Him. Because if you have a True relationship with Him, led by His Spirit within you, Loving your neighbor as yourself and upholding the law will just be a result of who you are because His Spirit will be yours. Remember, its no longer you who lives, but He lives in and through you."

I catch myself staring ahead, trying to follow along. I'm beginning to see the world from a brand new perspective. I see where things have been twisted, and I can see what my grand-pop must have understood.

I put my fingers up to the cross around my neck again, feeling more gratitude for what Jesus did for me and for God's grace and mercy than I ever have before. What Manny is saying is making total sense right now, and I want to live my life the way he's talking about.

But what if I don't always feel like this? What happens when I get back to my house and I can't even think straight over all the fear and negativity. What if I don't have enough faith to live like this?

PART FOUR

DEVELOPING FAITH

Chapter 14 - Taking a Test in School

We keep working our way toward the pond, and as we do, I take in the scenery. All the beautiful trees, people working on their gardens, and kids playing out in the front yard. It truly is a beautiful day.

"Are you good so far?" Manny asks.

"Actually, yes." I say, nodding my head. "It's definitely a lot to think about, but you're doing a good job making it simple. Thank you for that!"

"Well, thanks," Manny says. "Since we touched the surface of God's Love for us, we need to begin to check out faith, and I've got just the example for you. Students take tests all the time in school, right?"

"Unfortunately, yes," I say, although this quarantine has almost made me miss school enough to be okay with taking more tests.

"So they are taught to pay attention in class, study the teacher's notes consistently, and then they will be prepared for the test. When the test comes, they have the answers to the questions in their mind, and they release the answer from their mind and write it on the paper. This process is repeated until the test is finished. The students that panic are the ones that didn't study, study the wrong thing, or wait til the last minute, right?"

"Yup."

"Life, and our walk of faith, is just the same. We are given the Book (the Bible) to help us through Life. All of the answers are in there. We first spend time with the Word, study the Word consistently, until we 'know' (believe) the answers.[1] When we get tested, we are able to 'release' the answer by speaking out loud thru faith (belief in knowing the answer is correct).[2] The people that panic in life are the ones that do not study and do not spend time in the Word, study the wrong thing, or wait til the last minute.[3]

"So picture this: a class of 10 students was given a few weeks to study for a test. The teacher gave the students the book to study from, even taught them on the topics for a bunch of days, but said you won't be successful unless you consistently study the words in the book. The students nod their heads and depart from the classroom.

"The first two students dutifully follow the teacher's advice and do just what she suggested. The next two students decide they want to do well, but they choose to read another book that promises to help them succeed. Then there are four students who decide they don't want to read the book at all

---

[1] Romans 10:17
[2] Mark 11:22-24
[3] Hosea 4:6

because they've already come up with their own beliefs on what the answers to the test are."

"What about the last 2 students?" I ask.

"The last 2 students in this story do absolutely nothing, because they didn't believe the teacher was ever going to give a test in the first place."

"Sounds like some of my friends," I chuckle.

"So the day of the test comes, and guess what happens? The first two students who decided to follow the teachers advice did extremely well, both received good scores in the 90s and pleased the teacher."

"Makes sense," I say.

"The second two students, and the four students who neglected the teacher's advice, all failed the test. One group because they studied the wrong book and the other four because they decided they already knew the answers and had their own beliefs on what the answers were. As for the last two students that didn't believe the teacher and didn't think a test would come? They received 0% on the test. Now does any of that surprise you?"

"No, it doesn't surprise me" I say. "I knew exactly what was going to happen to the kids who didn't listen to the teacher."

"That's exactly the point," Manny says. "God has given us the Book to help us and teach us through Life. Through the power of His Spirit within us, if we speak in line with the word and meditate on it throughout the day and night, our words and actions will follow. A lot of the time people become distracted or just neglect the Book and wonder why they struggle spiritually, emotionally, mentally, socially, financially, or physically in life."

"It makes sense, but what does it have to do with faith?" I ask.

Chapter 15 - Faith is your Spiritual Muscle

"The Bible defines faith as the substance of things hoped for," Manny says, "and the evidence of things not seen.[1] It's like you're so confident in something you're hoping for, that you actually have physical evidence. That's how confident this form of belief is. And you acquire faith by hearing, and hearing by the Word of God."[2] Faith is a byproduct of His Spirit within you.[3]

"I always thought of faith as being, like, when you want something to be true but you just weren't sure."

"Let me describe faith another way," Manny says. "Faith is like our spiritual muscle. Just like when we are born, we are born with all of the muscles we will ever need. It just takes time and consistency to build those muscles to where we can crawl, stand, walk, run, pick up objects, and then eventually lift heavy things and become a strong young man like yourself."

---

[1] Hebrews 11:1
[2] Romans 10:17
[3] Galatians 5:22-23

***

"I don't know about that," I say under my breath, wondering when the last time was that someone called me strong. I'd started lifting weights last year and while I've seen some changes to my physique, they weren't coming as fast as I'd hoped.

"Well, the same thing happens when we accept Jesus as Lord and Savior. We are spiritually reborn and become infants again. When we accept Jesus as Lord and Savior, we are given His faith that lives and dwells on inside of us through His Holy Spirit, but it takes time and consistency to develop your faith in all of the promises of God.[4] Reason being, our mind needs to be transformed and renewed into the mind of Christ.[5] We are given His mind,[6] but we must constantly be renewing our mind into the His image to receive more of the gift of faith.[7]

"So it doesn't take any work on our part to be saved, but it does take work to develop faith?" I ask.

"That's right," Manny says. "Faith is a gift, but you can take that gift and work at it. And just like a physical muscle, developing spiritual muscle may take a short period of time for some and a longer period of time for others."

"That's funny," I say, "because I love lifting weights. I started last year but I haven't seen results as fast as I wanted."

***

---

[4] Psalms 1:1-4
[5] Romans 12:2
[6] 1 Corinthians 2:16
[7] Colossians 3:9-10

"Do you stick to a schedule or do you do lift whenever you feel like it?" He asks.

"Well, I sort of have a schedule," I say, "but I don't always stick to it."

"Well, just like with lifting weights, the goal of developing your spiritual muscle should be to stay consistent. I promise you, if you start getting consistent with both, you'll see your faith, and your arms, get bigger."

"So what's the workout plan, then?" I ask. "I've got a routine for the gym, but how can I develop my faith so that it's big and strong spiritually?"

"Great question," Manny smiles. "Just like developing physical muscle like your hamstrings, biceps, or abs, we can develop a plan for working out our spiritual muscle as well. It all begins with plugging in."

Chapter 16 - Plugging In

"Pull out your phone quick," Manny says, pointing to my pocket.

I reach into my pocket and pull it out, holding it up to see what he wants me to do with it.

"When you accept Jesus as Lord and Savior," he continues, "God has blessed you with His Grace (His Holy Spirit within you).[1] Essentially, you've been blessed with the Light of Life on the inside of you."[2]

The phone (you) now has light (His Spirit within you). Essentially, you're given all of the spiritual muscle (faith) you'll ever need."

Looking down at my phone, I click the side button and the phone illuminates.

"To charge the phone, the charger must be plugged into the

---

[1] Ephesians 1:13-14
[2] John 1:4

phone and into the outlet on the wall, right? The electricity is pulled from the power source, in this case the outlet, and transferred to the phone.

"For us to remain charged up in the Spirit, we must continue to plug into the Word of God and God will provide us with His power.[3]

"When it comes to the spiritual fitness analogy," Manny says, "spending time in God's Word is like going for a workout. There are numerous ways to spend time in His Word, just like there are many ways to workout.

"Ok, so I'm the phone and the way I charge myself is to plug into God?"

"Right," Manny says, "and the cord that connects us to God is His Word. The activity that is happening in the cord is the electricity. The electricity is the power pulled from the power source and transferred into the phone, which gives the phone 'light' and 'life'.

"When we plug into God (the Power Source) by the Word of God (the cord), the activity going on (electricity being transferred) is: believing, speaking,[4] and confessing the Word of God over your life[5] in a state of thankfulness.[6]

"You're essentially reading and/or praying in line with God's Word, declaring His Promises over your life, in a state of

---

[3] Joshua 1:8
[4] Mark 11:22-24
[5] Hebrews 10:23
[6] 1 Thessalonians 5:16-18

thankfulness. Does that make sense?"

"Yeah I think so," I say. "Basically, it's like finding these 'Promises' in the Bible and believing them by speaking them over your life, while being thankful for them?"

"Exactly," Manny smiles. "That's how you become charged up in the Spirit. THIS IS LIKE EXERCISING YOUR SPIRITUAL MUSCLE. The more you do this the stronger your faith becomes. In fact, how do you feel right now?"

"Really good, actually," I say because I do feel good. "This all makes sense and I'm starting to see how this stuff works."

"What you're experiencing right now is a form of that 'charged up' feeling," Manny says, "because a revelation has come to you. When you know the truth, the truth will set you free."[7]

"Now, eventually, you'll unplug your phone from the charger and the phone has energy. In regards to navigating or finding directions, the phone now has the power to be able to use the maps app to help you navigate to your destination.

"As we unplug from the Word of God, God provides us with energy to move throughout the day.[8] Although we are technically off of the charger, God empowers us with Christ's Holy Spirit within us.[9] By His Spirit within us, we are now able to navigate throughout the day and remain focused on

---

[7] John 8:31-32
[8] Philippians 4:13
[9] 1 Corinthians 15:10

Him by the power of His GPS — His Spirit within us."[10]

"Man, that's a really good analogy," I say. "I never thought of myself as a phone before."

"Speaking of your phone," Manny says, "do you need to touch base with your parents and let them know what you're up to? Maybe you should call them and tell them you've been walking around the neighborhood with one of your grandpop's old friends?"

"Nah, I'm good," I say. "My walks with Clark are always long, so they won't be worried about me. Besides, I feel like you're not done with this phone analogy, right?"

"Look at you," Manny says, "you're pretty perceptive! There is one more part of the analogy that needs to be addressed."

---

[10] Romans 8:14

Chapter 17 - The Uncharged Phone

"Has your phone ever died because it wasn't charged?" Manny asks.

"Yeah, a bunch of times," I say. "It's the worst."

"An uncharged phone cannot typically receive messages, unless by a miracle." Manny says. "Not only can an uncharged phone not see messages, it can't use the Maps app to help navigate, either. Imagine having to drive to a new place, five hours away, with no Maps app, and no actual map, just hoping to get there by luck?"

"My mom says people used to get lost all the time before GPS apps," I say.

"Yeah, technology has certainly changed a lot about life," Manny laughs. "And let me ask you this: what happens when your phone eventually turns back on?"

"I guess usually I have missed texts or calls," I answer.

"Right," Manny says. "Think of those missed messages as seeds that have been planted by the Word of God. And when we keep the phone on, we can directly communicate with our Father in Heaven, be aware of and led by His Guidance, and also be the Light for other people."

I hit the power button to put my phone back to sleep and slip it back in my pocket.

"How long will your phone last before it dies?" Manny asks.

"I don't know, probably another hour," I say.

"But eventually it will run out of energy and die without plugging into the power source, right?"

"Yeah, of course," I say.

"You see," Manny says, "it's common sense when it comes to our phones, but we often miss it when it comes to ourselves. We have to plug in consistently. Spending time praying to God is so important, but we have to also supplement that with getting plugged into His word to be charged up with His power."

"Really?" I say. "I figured spending a few minutes praying every day was good enough to let God know that I was thinking about him and wanted to make good choices."

"Remember, spending time with God is not about trying to convince Him of how you feel. He already knows your thoughts. Prayer, and reading the Bible, is about getting charged up by His power. All throughout the Bible, the Word says to meditate on His Word day and night; as a result, we will prosper (be successful) in all things."[1] If we do this our words and actions will fall in line God's will because we will be led by His Spirit.

"Wait," I stop him, "so you're telling me just by reading the Bible, God promises success?"

"Yes." Manny says. "Understanding what God has done for us, through His Son Jesus and His gift of the Holy Spirit, what do you think the ultimate form of success is?"

"I don't know," I say. "Seems like everyone is trying to be wealthy and happy, but I'm guessing that's not the kind of success you're talking about?"

"The ultimate form of success is Jesus manifesting Himself to us and through us." Manny says. "Jesus teaches He will do this to the ones that love Him; the ones who love Him keep His Word (teaching)[2]. That's why it's so important to plug into His Word daily. You'll continue renewing your mind[3] and becoming more rooted and grounded in His Love for you[4]; as a result, you'll be positioning yourself to allow God and Jesus to manifest themselves to you and through you.[5] How cool is that?"

"It sounds like a better life than a lot of people are living," I say.

* * *

---

[1] Joshua 1:8, Psalms 1:1-4
[2] John 14:19-24
[3] Romans 12:2
[4] Ephesians 3:17
[5] John 14:21

"Wealth and happiness aren't bad things, of course," Manny says, "but they can be fleeting. Here today and gone tomorrow. God wants us to be filled with joy, and he wants us to be a blessing to others as well. But those things should not be how we define success. In fact, Satan loves it when we define success that way because it can keep us distracted from being charged up and focusing on how much God loves us. Satan doesn't want us to grow into the Image of Jesus — because we will be dangerous to him! If he can keep us out of God's Word, we will never know who we are or the authority that God has given us through His Spirit within us."

"Wow," I remark, "I never knew plugging into God's Word was so important. Honestly, I never understood why people did. I thought people who read the Bible all the time were kind of goofy. I just didn't think it related to today because it's been around so long."

"I understand and have heard people say the same thing," Manny says, "But the Bible calls Jesus the Word that became flesh[6] and that Jesus (the Word) is the same yesterday, today, and forever[7]. We have to be careful with developing our own opinions, Satan can trick and deceive us there."

I guess I wasn't really sure where my opinion of the Bible had come from, but I was pretty sure it was never going to be the same again.

---

[6] John 1:14
[7] Hebrews 13:8

Chapter 18 - Knowing His Voice

"Okay maybe another dumb question," I say, "but plugging into God through His Word. Is it really as simple as just opening the Bible and reading? It seems so simple to have that much of an effect."

"Not a dumb question at all," Manny says. "If you don't truly read God's Word, you miss out on hearing what His voice sounds like.[1] If we are unaware of what God's Voice sounds like, we can mistake the enemy's voice either telling us lies or more dangerously, telling us half-truths;[2] because half-truths sound like the truth, but at their core they are deceptions.

"For people that have some religious or spiritual background and have been taught the basics, but don't keep their focus on reading the Word daily (hearing His voice daily), those people will get crossed up between half-truths and lies because their mind hasn't been transformed by the whole Truth and they mistake Satan's voice for God's voice occasionally.

---

[1] John 10:25-30
[2] John 8:44

***

"Think of it like this: a young Christian person struggles with self image, doesn't think they are good-looking and/or doesn't feel loved. They get a lot of negative thoughts going through their mind throughout the day and it wears on them. Know any kids like that?"

"Yeah, it sounds like how I might describe a few people I know." I say.

"Well," Manny says, "if they really knew how much God loves them and how He sees them, they would be experiencing so much more love, joy, and peace in their lives;[3] because that's a byproduct of who He is within you."[4]

"The Word says the enemy is coming to steal, kill, and destroy.[5] What do you think He is trying to steal?"

"I don't know," I say, "our joy or happiness?"

"He is coming to steal the Word."[6] Manny corrects me. "He knows if you're cut off from hearing the Truth, seeing yourself how God's sees you and how much He loves you, you'll never find out the power and authority God has given you in this earth over Satan and evil.[7] So if Satan steals the Word, he knows he can destroy your life, and eventually lead you to sin and death."[8]

---

[3] John 14:27-29
[4] Galatians 5:22-23
[5] John 10:10
[6] Matthew 13:19
[7] Luke 10:19
[8] James 1:13-15

* * *

"So wait," I say, feeling a few things click together with Manny's analogy. "Satan doesn't have the power to mess with God, who is the power source, so instead, he tries to steal our power cord - which is God's Word - so that we can't get charged up and we won't know God's voice?"

"You nailed it." Manny says.

Chapter 19 - The Eye is the Lamp

My jaw must be touching the pavement right now, because this makes so much sense.

"Woah. Sir, you have no idea how much this hits home. I used to get picked on in school and I felt insecure because I never thought I was 'good' enough."

"I completely understand." Manny says gently. "Many young people go through things that are very similar to what you described. If young people knew how much God loved them and how He sees them, they would be in such a state of love, joy, and peace.[1] People try to achieve those things on their own, but God has made it easy for them; they just have to spend time in His Word, seeing His Love, and seeing themselves how God sees them.[2]

"Let me ask you this," Manny says. "Jesus taught that the Eye was the lamp of the body[3], what does that mean to you?"

---

[1] John 14:27-29
[2] John 14:23-24
[3] Matthew 6:22-23

* * *

'Umm...that's kind of a weird thing to say," I respond. "But, I guess it probably means that when you look in someone's eyes, you can sorta tell what state they're in."

"You can definitely tell where someone is based on their eyes," Manny says, "but the question becomes, why can you tell where they are at by looking at their eyes? This story is all about perception, how we see things. If you see the world from the proper perspective, you will be full of Light.[4] If you see things from the wrong perspective, you will be full of darkness.[5]

"Think of someone that is extremely negative, they always see the worst in every situation. It's truly sad because they are typically in a bad mood because they don't feel good themselves; it weighs on them and not many people enjoy being around them for long periods of time. Now think of a positive person, always cheery and sees the best in every situation. People are drawn to that type of person. Even in the midst of chaos, they seem to find the opportunity and good in every situation."

"I totally get that," I say, with a few people coming to mind for each example. I definitely like being around the positive people more than the negative ones.

As I think about that idea, we walk past one of my favorite houses in our neighborhood. The front yard has two massive oak trees with the house sitting behind them. It's an old stone house with ivy growing up the one side of the house and

---

[4] Matthew 6:22
[5] Matthew 6:23

massive windows in the front. They've got a big long driveway, as well. Every time I walk by the house I always stare and admire it.

"Nice house right?" Manny says. "Beautiful, old, classic in every way."

"It's one of my favorite houses," I say.

"Or is it rundown, in need of updating, and not very modern?" Manny asks. "It depends on your perspective, right? When you continue filling your mind with "Light," aka The Word,[6] it'll change your perspective and how you see the world. You'll begin seeing Love. You'll begin speaking Love and Faith,[7] not fear, stress, worry, hatred, self-doubt, and pride . You'll then be able to be the light for others in a world that's full of negativity and darkness."[8]

"Pull your phone out of your pocket and wake it up, so I can tie this together," Manny says. I do what he asks and the first thing it does is light up.

"Your phone is on because it's charged, and it's charged because you recently plugged it in to the power source. When we plug into the Word of God, we give God the opportunity to charge us up Spiritually, which trickles down into how we see, think, feel, etc. The goal is to have our senses trained to follow our spirit, not the other way around.

"When we continually plug into His Word and then are

---

[6] John 8:12, John 1:14
[7] Luke 6:43-45
[8] Romans 12:1-2

removed from His Word going about living out our day physically, we still are charged up with His Power through His Spirit within us that can help us navigate through life and more effectively communicate with Him."

"I feel like my life is going to get better because of this," I say.

"And the best part is, not only did He put this system in place for you, but this perfect system has been put in place so you can then be a Light and give direction for others, as well.

"Think of Love and faith like this," Manny continues, "love is giving — God so loved the world that He gave.[9] Faith is like receiving[10] — receiving what God has given us. We receive God's Love by faith, and we live a life led by love by giving ourselves to God and giving Love to other people."

"I can't tell you how much better I feel than when I left the house," I say. "This all makes so much sense. One thing I just thought of, though. What about going to church? Is that another way to plug in?"

"Absolutely," Manny says. "Church services, listening to a sermon, singing along with worship music, study and prayer time on your own are all ways to connect with God's Word. Anytime you're mindfully in the Word you are connecting to the power source and getting charged up."

We come to a stop sign and I'm so lost in the conversation that I'm not sure which way we should go.

* * *

---

[9] John 3:16-17
[10] Romans 4:13-25

"Let's turn right here and start making our way back to your house," Manny says. "There are a couple more things I want to share with you before we get you back."

PART FIVE

WHO GOD
SAYS YOU ARE

Chapter 20 - Where to Plug in First?

As we walk towards the corner house that's a couple hundred yards away from the pond, I'm blown away by the course this day has taken. I started the day upset and sick of being home, then Clark almost got hit by a truck, and now I'm learning so much and beginning to understand what my grand-pop not only understood, but lived out. This might be the most bizarre day ever.

"Okay, I've got a question for you," I say, "The Bible is such a big book, and typically in books, you start from page one. But it seems like with the Bible, people jump around all over the place. So if I want to start plugging in, where should I start?"

"Fantastic question." Manny says. "If and when people grasp this answer, it will change their life. It's really a simple truth. If someone already has a small bit of background and has accepted Jesus as Lord and Savior, I do have a recommendation.

"Remember, the tree example? It's about becoming rooted and grounded in God's Love. You become rooted and grounded in God's Love by seeing His Word from the perspective of how much He loves you and how He sees you[1] — which is one of the most important fundamentals when reading scripture.

"Can you say that again?"

"Essentially, this is how faith and love work together: Faith doesn't work when there is fear or doubt.[2] As soon as you can let go of fear and doubt, faith can work. The easy part is, perfect love drives out fear,[3] so if you become rooted and grounded in God's Love,[4] the faith that God has given you through His Spirit within you will have the ability to work and produce incredible results; because faith works by love.[5] So when you develop your faith in God's Love for you, it's a perfect system and you can become the tree that produces His type of fruit.[6]

"What do you mean, the faith God has given you?" I ask.

"Remember the fruit of the Spirit, which is the result of His presence within you. One of those fruits is faith[7]. Therefore, faith is a byproduct of living by the Spirit, because of who Christ is within you."

"Got it," I say. " I want to be that kind of tree that produces that kind of fruit."

---

[1] Ephesians 3:14-21
[2] James 1:6-8
[3] 1 John 4:18
[4] Ephesians 3:17
[5] Galatians 5:6
[6] Galatians 5:22-23
[7] Galatians 5:22-23

***

"I can tell that you do," Manny says. "The goal is simple, really; it's to become rooted and grounded in God's Love (develop your faith in God's Love for you), so you can become Love. When you do that, Love is just a result of who you are, because it's who He is within you."[8]

Manny pauses on the edge of the road, just before we reach the grass area in front of the pond, he puts his finger on my heart.

"Remember that Holy Spirit that's right here? Remember, it's no longer you who lives, it's His Spirit that lives within you.[9] The works (loving others, giving to others, being the light for others, etc.) are just a byproduct of who you are, because of who He is within you.[10]

He pauses for a second and then continues. "I know I didn't fully answer your question yet, but that's the rough gist of it. If you're really interested, I can show you exactly how to develop your faith muscle/plug into His Love for you."

"I am," I say.

We walk across the small field and make our way to the pond. Clark rushes towards the water, dragging me with him. Manny can't help but laugh as I nearly fall in the pond, slipping on fresh mud.

Since I don't feel like fighting him, I just let Clark off of the

---

[8] 2 Corinthians 3:18
[9] Galatians 2:20
[10] 1 Corinthians 15:10, Galatians 5:22-23, Galatians 5:16

leash and allow him to splash around in the water. Boxers don't really like the water, but we got him used to it when he was a pup. Although he still doesn't really like to swim in deep water, he genuinely likes the splashing around now.

Stepping away from Clark, I look back at my new friend, who is taking his last sip of water. I can tell he's about to say something.

"If you were to grasp and take away ONE thing from the Bible and live by it, what would that be?" He asks me.

"To love your neighbor as yourself? The Golden Rule."[11] I answer.

"Good answer," Manny says approvingly, "but what would make that easy? What would make that effortlessly possible?"

"Before this conversation, I would have been clueless." I say. "But now I actually think I know. It's possible when you live by His Spirit within you, right?"

"That's right!" Manny says with a huge smile. "Yes, if you were to live by the Spirit, you will not carry out the desires of sinful nature (the flesh).[12] You see, if you were to live by the Spirit, you would only be able to produce the fruit of the Spirit — love, joy, peace, patience, kindness, goodness, faithfulness, gentleness, and self-control; because the fruit of the Spirit is the result of His presence within you.[13]

---

[11] Mark 12:28-34
[12] Galatians 5:16-17
[13] Galatians 5:22-23

* * *

"You see, because of the finished work of the cross, (what Jesus has done for us), we now have His Spirit that lives and dwells in our hearts,[14] if we learn to live by the Spirit, the fruit of the Spirit will be a result — because of His presence within us. And Love just happens to be the first fruit mentioned."

"It's so cool that He made it easy for us," I say, "but wait, how do I learn to live by the Spirit? Like, what does that actually mean?"

---

[14] Ephesians 1:13-14

Chapter 21 - Become Transformed

Looking back at Clark splashing around in the water and running up and down the bank, Manny says, "The Holy Spirit that lives and dwells on the inside of you must become your identity.[1]

"In other words, we must begin to see ourselves how God sees us. And as that picture becomes more clear, through meditating on God's Word and seeing His Love for us, we will realize our new identity in Christ."

"But I'm not gonna be perfect all the time, I just know it." I say.

"Not, you won't," Manny says. "All the more reason for your identity to be in Christ, who lives in you. And the only way for the Spirit to become your identity is by renewing your mind, completely transforming your mind to the Mind

---

[1] Romans 8:29, 2 Corinthians 3:18, Colossians 3:9-10

of Christ,[2] which we have been given.[3]

"As a follower of Christ," he continues, "we must have our minds renewed and transformed by 'plugging into' (meditating) on the Word of God constantly,[4] specifically the finished work of the cross (The promises of our New Identity in Christ). And as a result, we won't be trained by the world, but we will actually be trained by the Word[5] to think with the Mind of Christ.[6] We will train our minds to see ourselves how God sees us, and we'll live in a more Christ-like way as a result."

"Seriously, that sounds great," I say, feeling the pressure lifted off of my shoulders, "But you still didn't tell me where I should begin in the Bible."

"We'll get there," he smiles. "I love that you're into this. You know, when you become a new believer, when you accept Jesus as a Lord and Savior, you're given His Holy Spirit. Spiritually, the old you has passed away, and the new you is born[7] — His Holy Spirit within you.[8] When that happens, you want to figure out your new identity — your identity in Him.[9]

* * *

---

[2] Romans 12:2
[3] 1 Corinthians 2:16, Philippians 2:5
[4] Joshua 1:8, Psalms 1:1-4, Romans 12:2
[5] Romans 12:2
[6] 1 Corinthians 2:16
[7] 2 Corinthians 5:17
[8] Galatians 2:20
[9] Colossians 3:1-3, 9-10

"The question becomes, what does your identity in Him look like? Or simply stated, how does God see you? In the Bible, there are roughly 140 verses that tell us who we are in Him — this essentially means, like I've said before, how much God loves us and how He sees us in Christ. Remember the goal, to become rooted and grounded in God's Love[10] (your identity found in God's Love for you, which is the finished work of the cross).

"The identity verses are a good starting point to begin to see the power of the finished work of the cross. The identity verses are God's Love for us. When you read these verses, see them as God talking to you, that His Word is final,[11] and that this is how much He loves you. Those words are meant to become your new identity.[12] God loves us so much, He saved us from our old self, which was directly connected to sin and death, and gave us a brand new identity — His Holy Spirit.[13] The same exact Spirit that Jesus has. Also, when you read these verses, read the verses around them as well so you can interpret the meaning through the context of what's written around it.

"Once we begin praying and believing for what those verses are telling us we are, we will be praying/speaking in line with His Word, which is the Will of God, which activates our faith. If we believe we receive it, we will have it.

"Okay...identity verses," I say. "Can you give me an example?"

---

[10] Ephesians 3:17
[11] 2 Corinthians 1:20
[12] Romans 8:29, 2 Corinthians 3:18
[13] Romans 8:2, 2 Corinthians 5:17

***

"Absolutely," Manny says. "For instance, Mark 11:22-24 in the Amplified Bible where Jesus is giving us specific directions to activate the faith He has given us through His Holy Spirit. It says,

"Jesus replied, "Have faith in God [constantly]. I assure you and most solemnly say to you, whoever says to this mountain, 'Be lifted up and thrown into the sea!' and does not doubt in his heart [in God's unlimited power], but believes that what he says is going to take place, it will be done for him [in accordance with God's will]. For this reason I am telling you, whatever things you ask for in prayer [in accordance with God's will], believe [with confident trust] that you have received them, and they will be given to you."

"Wow, that's good stuff," I say.

"It is," Manny says. "These verses are so important. Honestly, we could spend hours talking about this topic, but maybe we'll save this whole idea of 'living by faith' for our next walk."

"I would love that." I say, trying not to sound too excited. "What would a session look like if I were to do this on my own? How would I go about receiving God's Promises? How would I go about renewing my mind, to the point where I see myself how God sees me."

"Again, it's so simple," Manny says, "No need to make this complicated. Simply put, read and meditate on the Word. Then, begin to confess the Word (the promise of God) as

YOURS in a state of thankfulness.[14] Some people like to highlight their Bible. Some people like to write it down as well.

"For example, I've seen people highlight these verses in one specific color, so when they flip through their Bible, the identity verses are easily spotted. That's one way to do it."

Manny picks up a stick and tosses it in the edge of the pond, where Clark dive bombs the stick, and races back to drop it at his feet. They repeat this over and over again, and it makes me wonder how many times they've done this before together and I just never knew.

---

[14] 1 Thessalonians 5:16-18

Chapter 22 - Receiving God's Love and Praying in line with His will

"You like receiving Christmas gifts?" Manny asks.

"Um, of course," I say.

"Well, receiving God's Promises is a lot like being a kid on Christmas. You know, as a kid you'd run downstairs on Christmas morning and find gifts underneath and around the Christmas tree. All of the gifts were wrapped; which made the morning all the more fun, because you didn't know exactly what was inside the wrapping paper.

"God's Promises are like those gifts, in that they are wrapped. How do we unwrap those gifts? We unwrap those gifts by opening up His Word and reading them. As we begin seeing what those gifts are, it's up to us to receive it.

"Everyone loves gifts," I say.

Right," Manny says, "and what do you do when you receive a gift?"

* * *

My thoughts jump back to a time when I was younger, remembering the excitement I'd have opening presents. "I'd jump around and say 'THANK YOU SANTA!' At the top of my lungs," I laughed.

"Exactly right! Just like those gifts from Santa, you receive God's Gifts and Promises the same way. We thank Him for what He has done for us and what He has given us. When you thank Him[1], it puts you in a state of humility, faith, and hope, because it keeps your focus on Him and what He has done for you. When we see those gifts and promises from God from the perspective of 'This is how much God loves me and how God sees me,' you'll become rooted and grounded in His Love.[2]

"Remember, faith works by love.[3] Now, your faith will be working by the power and strength of His perfect love for you.[4] You see, this cycle is perfect and super simple! You just have to learn how to use it, which you are right now!"

"It does seem easy!" I say, feeling filled with joy. "So amazing and so simple as well. I receive God's love, aka His promises, by thanking Him for it, which puts me in a state of faith and hope. All of that helps me see life with a perspective of how much God loves me, which empowers the faith He has given me, which then gives me the ability to receive it. Woah man, this is a deep, but simple truth."

"You got it!" He smiles. "Love is like giving. Faith is like

---

[1] 1 Thessalonians 5:16-18
[2] Ephesians 3:17
[3] Galatians 5:6
[4] Ephesians 6:10, Philippians 4:13

receiving. God so loved you that He gave His only begotten Son for you.[5] You see, God is a giver. There are so many gifts He has given and wants to continuing giving His children[6], and remember all believers are accepted into God's family as children.[7] God wants to give us all of Himself, but we must receive what He has given us by faith.[8] Also, keep in mind, continue seeking the Giver," as he points up to heaven, "the gifts are a byproduct. That should make sense in a little bit."

"Can you show me what receiving His gifts and promises looks like?" I ask. I'm not so worried if my questions are dumb anymore, because Manny seems to have great answers for everything.

"Let's take these two verses for example," he says. "Both of these verses can be relatable with what's going on in the world today with the coronavirus pandemic. Second Timothy 1:7 in the NKJV says 'For God has not given us a spirit of fear, but of power and of love and of a sound mind.'

"And then in First John 4:18 it says, '"There is no fear in love; but perfect love casts out fear, because fear involves torment. But he who fears has not been made perfect in love'."

"So, after we read those," Manny says, "let's begin to pray in line with them. And let's say you're reading this when you feel fear trying to creep in, this is how you could pray:

"Father, I thank you so much for loving me. I thank you for

---

[5] John 3:16-17
[6] Ephesians 1:3-7, Galatians 3:29
[7] John 1:12-13, Ephesians 1:5, Galatians 3:26-27, Galatians 4:6-7
[8] Mark 11:22-24

not giving me a spirit of fear! I thank you for giving me a spirit of Power, Love, and of a sound mind. And father, I thank you for there being NO FEAR IN LOVE. Father, you love me so much that you put your perfect love in my heart, Your Holy Spirit. And Father, I thank you for your perfect love casting out the fear that I am feeling right now. I thank you for loving me, and I receive your love right now, in Jesus' Name, Amen.

"Okay, I get it now," I say, feeling like my jaw is on the floor again. "I definitely have never prayed like that before in my life."

"Well, now's the perfect time to start," Manny says. "When you pray in line with God's Word (which is His Will), you're thanking Him for it. The Bible says we need to give thanks in everything, which is the will of God in Christ Jesus for you,[9] and you're declaring it over your life.[10]

"When you see it from the perspective of this is how much God loves you, that's a way for that "perfect love to cast out the fear." The more time you put into prayer and study time in the Word, you'll be able to tie in more verses and promises together — which can make that more powerful."

"So that's what you mean by developing your faith muscle and plugging in?!" I say.

"I think he's getting it," Manny says to Clark, while rubbing his belly.

* * *

---

[9] 1 Thessalonians 5:16-18
[10] Mark 11:22-24

He's right. I think I am.

Chapter 23 - Reflections

Clark pops up when he's had enough of the belly rub from Manny and starts rolling in the mud by the edge of the pond.

"Oh Clark," I say, "not the mud!"

It's kind of funny to watch, but for a few seconds I'm slightly annoyed that I'm gonna have to bathe him later. Then I catch myself complaining and having a bad attitude and I thank God for blessing me with such a great pup.

"Here's the important thing with all this," Manny says, "when you begin to deny yourself — essentially meaning when you no longer see yourself as 'you,' but 'Christ that lives in you,' these promises begin to become more alive in your life. Jesus sacrificed Himself so He could put His Spirit within you so that you could have what/who He is and what He has.[1]

"In this example, you could just experience Love and not fear! He went to the cross so you didn't have to deal with

---

[1] Ezekiel 36:25-32, John 14:15-18

fear, because through Him you are a conqueror and an overcomer.[2] But if you don't know that or develop your faith in that promise that is found in the Word, Satan will beat you up with fear all day long.[3] We just have to get out of our own way, and let God take over!"

Manny's words hit me hard because I've heard them before. I look down, thinking about all of the times where I screwed up in sports. My buddies used to make fun of me because I never seemed to come through when the game was on the line.

"Funny you say that," I say, looking up at him. "I struggle a lot with getting out of my own way. I've had my parents, coaches, and everyone tell me, 'I just needed to get out of my own way' so many times. Honestly, I try to, but I have no idea how to do that."

"I want you to look at your reflection in the pond." Manny says. "What do you see?"

"I see me."

"Yep. Absolutely. Now when you look at your reflection, I want you to begin moving side to side. Try to move past yourself."

"Yeah, I physically can't." I say. "Every way I move, I'm right there in the way to stop me."

"Exactly right," he says. "When you're constantly focused on

---

[2] John 16:33, 1 John 5:4-5, Romans 8:37, 1 John 4:4
[3] Hosea 4:6

yourself it's impossible to get out of your own way. The only way you can truly get out of your own way is by putting your complete focus on Him.[4] He frees you from you.[5] When you see Him and are prioritizing your focus on Him, you are not focusing on yourself or the problems you might have had.

"When you are truly focused on Him, the 'reflection of yourself' is moved away, and you're able to continue on your way on the path toward God because you now see His light. Your eye can only truly look at or intently focus on ONE thing at a time. It's up to you to decide where we are looking."

I had never thought of it like that before, but it was so true. I look back down to the water and my reflection stares back at me through the ripples.

"You see," he says, "it's all about denying yourself, picking up your cross, and following me."[6]

I didn't catch it at first, but a few seconds later my brain realizes what he had said. "...following me." It hits me all at once and every hair on my body suddenly stands on end.

I look up and I realize it's really Him. Jesus.

I collapse right to the ground, not believing what I'm seeing. Lord, is this really You? Am I dreaming?

His hand touches my shoulder and he says, "I AM. Rise up,

---

[4] Isaiah 26:3
[5] John 8:32
[6] Matthew 16:24-25

son."

I stand up, completely astonished and overwhelmed, but as I look in His eyes, I feel at peace and at home. I feel His Love and I hug Him, feeling so sorry for ever doubting Him and being upset with Him in the past.

"I love you." He says, embracing me. "I forgive you. Stop looking at what's behind you. It's in the past.[7] I'm here, now. Let's walk."

He knew every thought that I had, I didn't have to say a word. Just His Words and gentle smile comforted me.

"Wait, you said your name was Manny," I say. "Were you lying to me?"

"I said, 'you can call me Manny'" Jesus says. "Short for Emmanuel, which is one of my names. It means 'God with us'.

I put the pup back on the leash and we start walking again. Emmanuel. God with Us. And Jesus is literally with me right now; I'm still not sure if I believe it. I'm walking with my Lord and Savior, Jesus, the Son of God. Is this really happening? If it is, he probably knows exactly what I'm thinking right now, which is probably why He's smiling.

I find myself at a loss for words for quite a while, but eventually a question pops into my head.

"Lord, what's going on with this virus right now?" I ask.

---

[7] Hebrews 10:16-17, Phillippians 3:12-16

"And all of the other problems and issues in the world? So many people are freaking out, scared, and worried. What's going on?"

"When you saw Me and came close to Me, what did you feel?"

"I felt at peace, I felt at home, I felt Your Love."

"As we are talking now, what are you experiencing?"

"All the same." I said. "I feel like the whole world has stopped. I feel at such peace, so much love, completely joy and happiness."

"You see, just like the mirror, when people focus on themselves and their current situation or what's going in the world around them, their peace can get compromised. When you continue to keep your eyes on Me, God will keep you in peace.[8] Our Love will cast out fear from your life.[9] You will experience Our Presence.[10] When you focus on Our Love for you, you'll become rooted and grounded in Our Love,[11] living by Our Spirit that lives right here will be a result."[12]

Jesus puts His hand on my heart and it all makes sense. Everything clicks.

He puts His hand on my heart where He put His Spirit,

---

[8] Isaiah 26:3
[9] 1 John 4:18
[10] John 14:19-24, Galatians 5:22-23
[11] Ephesians 3:17
[12] 2 Corinthians 3:18, Galatians 5:22-23

showing me that's where He is; that's where He is living.

Sometimes you're so close to something you can't see it, that's sort of like His Spirit. It's so close to you, sometimes you can't see it or even look past it.

Chapter 24 - Knowing Me

We walk around the corner to my street probably about 10 houses away from mine, and all I can think is "thank goodness these houses have big yards! This is so cool! I'm walking with Jesus!"

We stroll past a middle aged couple, and they hardly acknowledge us, which catches me by surprise. It seems like they were busy in conversation.

A few moments later, a car slowly drives by us and I think for sure it's going to stop and the guy inside is going to cause a scene. But he didn't. He was on the phone and didn't even wave.

"What is going on here?" I finally say. "I'm literally walking with Jesus and no one else is even waving at You? Am I in my own little world right now dreaming all of this or is this real?"

"They don't recognize Me because they don't know Me."[1] Jesus

---

[1] Matthew 7:21-24, John 17:3

says.

Hearing Him speak those words stills my heart. "Lord, what do you mean they don't know You?" I ask.

"The guy driving by in the car is so distracted by what's going on in his world: his job, his travels, his money, and material success, that he let that take priority in His heart.[2] He went to church growing up, but never developed that relationship with Me. He went to college and got distracted by all of the 'temporary and short-lived' pleasures, made some bad decisions, and figured out life on his own. Because of his personal will-power, he has found material success in his career and finances, but has lost his way with his family and has turned from our relationship, unknowingly."

"Oh my goodness," I say, "What about the married couple?"

"They go to church every Sunday, but they haven't taken the time to get to know Me; to have an intimate relationship with Me and God the Father;[1] knowing Us is eternal life.[3] I love people dedicated to celebrating a service in My Name every week, but the question becomes, what about the other 167 hours per week? God and I desire a relationship with each one of you[4] through the Holy Spirit which We have given you."

"Lord, how do I make sure I'm developing that relationship with you?"

* * *

---

[2] Matthew 6:24
[3] John 17:3
[4] John 1:10-13, 1 Timothy 2:4

"Go into your most private room, close the door, and pray to your Father in Heaven.[5] Spend time with God and me, and don't do it to make a scene so you can seen by others.

"Spend time in the Word to get to know Me, because I am the Word that became flesh.[6] Practice seeing the entire Bible from the perspective of this is how much We love you. Practice seeing Me in every Book, in every Chapter, in every Verse, and in every Word.

"Use what you have learned so far and what I am about to explain to you."

---

[5] Matthew 6:6
[6] John 1:1-4, John 1:14

Chapter 25 - Knowing Christ is in You

Jesus continues, "There's a question that you haven't thought of that I'd like to ask you. How do you know that My Spirit lives within you?

Scratching the back of my head, I answer, "I'm not sure."

"I've said this in the third chapter of the Gospel according to John when I was speaking with Nicodemus, 'unless one is born again, he cannot see the kingdom of God.'[1] What is the Kingdom of God?"

"Your Spirit within me?"[2]

"Very good! I follow that comment up with, 'unless one is born of water and the Spirit, he cannot enter the kingdom of God. That which is born of the flesh is flesh, and that which is born of the Spirit is spirit. Do not marvel that I said to you, 'You must be born again.'[3]

---

[1] John 3:3
[2] Luke 17:20-21
[3] John 3:5-7

***

"Some religions don't agree with that or just have their own way of saying it. Simply put, it's a spiritual rebirth. We wipe your slate completely clean, with My blood that was shed when I was condemned and put to death."[4]

"Okay," I add, "What do you mean 'born again?'"

"Truly being born again, essentially living a born again life, is repenting of your sins (asking forgiveness and completely turning away from sin[5]) by living through My spirit within you, and giving your life to God.[6] For God so loved the world that He gave His only begotten Son (Me), that whoever believes in Me should not perish but have everlasting life.[7] For God did not send Me into the world to condemn the world, but that the world through Me might be saved.[8] When you confess with your mouth that I am your Lord and Savior and believe in your heart that God has raised Me from the dead, you will be saved."[9]

Looking down at the pup, I try to soak this all in.

Jesus continues, "Think of it like this, because of Adam and Eve, the entire world was born into a spiritual disease. Resulting in spiritual death. The spiritual disease is 'sin.' When you confess with your mouth that I am your Lord and Savior and believe in your heart that God has raised Me from

---

[4] Ephesians 1:7, 2 Corinthians 5:17, Hebrews 10:16-17, Hebrews 10:10
[5] Acts 3:19, Acts 3:10-26
[6] Galatians 2:20, Matthew 16:24-25
[7] John 3:16
[8] John 3:17
[9] Romans 10:9

the dead, you will be saved.[8] I gave My life on the cross for you to forgive you from sin, so you never have to go to Hell. God raised Me from the dead to justify you[10] — to make you righteous."[11]

"Wow, could you explain that last part again?"

Smiling, Jesus nods His head. "I was raised from the dead, so God could justify you. In other words, make you righteous (being seen as right in God's eyes"). Remember, that sin disease that you were born into because of Adam and Eve? We removed you from that and completely healed you of your sin disease.[12] Your new health is righteousness — which comes from my Holy Spirit within you.[13] When you believed in Me as your personal Savior, We sealed you with the gift of My Spirit.[14] In summary, the Holy Spirit within you makes you right with God, or righteous.[15] God doesn't see you as a sinner anymore.

"The more you begin to develop your faith in having been made righteous because of My Spirit within you,[16] you'll see and appreciate the Love We have for you more. Also, you will remain humble and realize that the salvation that took place isn't from something you earned, but it was a gift from

---

[10] Romans 4:25
[11] 2 Corinthians 5:21
[12] 2 Corinthians 5:17, Titus 3:4-7
[13] 2 Corinthians 5:21
[14] Ephesians 1:13-14
[15] 2 Corinthians 5:21
[16] Romans 1:17, Romans 10:10

God."[17]

"That's really deep," I say, "but it does make a lot of sense. We were made right with God so we could also spend eternity with You in heaven?"[18]

"Absolutely," Jesus nods, "But don't think of it only for that. You were made right with God so you could come boldly to the Father and have an intimate relationship with Him now, through the Holy Spirit within you.[19] You were given a righteous spirit to produce heaven on this earth, by who I am within you."[20]

"This is so amazing how this entire conversation is coming full circle from the beginning of our walk in the garden."

"Remember, this has nothing to do with religion. You can be born again when you accept me as your Personal Lord and Savior. When you confess Me as your Lord and Savior and believe that God has raised Me from the dead, you will be saved.[8]

"I want you to hear an awesome verse from the book of Galatians that The Holy Spirit wrote through Paul. It's Galatians 2:20 and the Amplified version says:

"I have been crucified with Christ [that is, in Him I have shared His crucifixion]; it is no longer I who live, but Christ lives in me. The life I now live in the body I live by faith [by

---

[17] Titus 3:4-7, Ephesians 2:8-9
[18] John 3:16-17
[19] Hebrews 4:16
[20] Galatians 5:16-17, Galatians 5:22-23

adhering to, relying on, and completely trusting] in the Son of God, who loved me and gave Himself up for me."

"That is so good and so powerful," I say. "I've got to read that more tonight when I get home."

"I hope you do," Jesus says. "Remember, it's about denying yourself, completely trusting God and learning to live by My Spirit within you. We want to produce heaven on earth through you. By identifying yourself with My Spirit within you, We will cause you to walk in Our ways.[21] We are Love.[22] Thus, You are Love, because We have made Our home within you."[23]

"Okay, I think the light bulb just went off!" I say. "So we were born with a sin disease because of Adam and Eve. You came to the world and gave up Your life to save us and essentially purify us from that sin disease; so we can spend eternity with You in heaven, but also produce heaven on this earth while we are still here. And the way we start that process is by accepting You as our Lord and Savior and believing God has raised you from the dead. When we believe in You and repent of our sins, turning away from them, we are spiritually born again."

"You got it!" Jesus nods. "Also, if you do slip up and sin, come before God and ask forgiveness. He will forgive you and you'll be made clean."[24]

* * *

---

[21] Ezekiel 36:27
[22] 1 John 4:8
[23] John 14:23
[24] 1 John 1:9

"And once we have been spiritually reborn," I continue, "we are removed from that sin disease and purified with righteousness. Which, essentially, is a gift from God that makes us holy and blameless in His eyes."

"That's right," Jesus smiles. "Picture that righteousness as a pure, white cloak.[25] Are you putting it on?"

I can tell he wants me to keep talking, so I continue, "Okay, yeah, so I am wearing this white cloak, which symbolizes righteousness, which is given to me from God. Now, we are able to come close to God, boldly, because He doesn't see us as sinners anymore, because of Your Spirit within us, aka that white cloak."

"Excellent!" Jesus says, nodding along.

"So because of the brand new, reborn spirit within me, I am now given the ability to live a 'Christ-like' life," I say, looking into Jesus' kind and gentle eyes. "By your Spirit I can live a life like You and produce heaven on this earth while I am here."

"Like I told you earlier," Jesus says, "it's all about becoming the tree. You are the seed. When you are rooted and grounded in our Father's Love, by truly knowing how much We Love you,[26] your faith will begin to develop in His Love for you, and by faith you (the seed/tree) can grow[27]. Then you will produce Our fruit: Love, Joy, Peace, Patience, Kindness,

---

[25] Revelation 19:8
[26] Ephesians 3:14-21
[27] Romans 1:17, 2 Corinthians 3:18

Goodness, Faithfulness, Gentleness, and Self-Control.[28] People will be able to experience the fruit of My Spirit within you, just by your actions, the words that you speak, and how you speak them.[29]

"Look at this tree," He continues. "Look how tall and magnificent it is. Note how wide the tree is, how many branches it has, and the thousands of leaves it produces; all of this tree's beauty stems from what is happening right underneath our feet, in the soil. The seed was once this tiny, and see when planted in the proper soil, it can grow to be so magnificent. ITS ALL ABOUT THE ROOTS IN THE GROUND. The roots bring the nutrients to the tree. Stay rooted and grounded in Our Love, and you'll grow into a tree just like this one. Strive to grow deeper into Our Love every single day."

"I want to do that Jesus," I say, "and I'm sure others do, too. But why do people, even when they are spiritually reborn, still struggle or don't live a life like You?"

"Spiritually, the battle is won." He responds. "The battle that people are in is a soul battle — in the mind, the will, and the emotions. If who you are spiritually doesn't match how your mind sees you, you'll become deceived and will get beaten up by the enemy.[30] That's where fear, worry, stress, sickness, etc comes in and can hurt you.[31] That's why staying consistent, meditating in Our Words, constantly throughout

---

[28] Galatians 5:22-23
[29] Luke 6:43-45
[30] 3 John 3:2-4
[31] Hosea 4:6

the day is so important.[32] That's why constantly praying and confessing your new identity is so important.[33] It keeps your focus on Us. Keep your focus on God and I through the power of Our Spirit within you and Our Words, we will direct your path."[34]

"Trust in God, and He will guide you. I've heard my grand-pop say that so many times."

"Amen, starting to connect the dots?"

"Oh my yes, absolutely. So wait, You said You knew my grandfather. You said you walked with Him a lot?"

"Yes, we are very good friends," Jesus says. "Your grandfather gave His life to Me many years ago. We walked everyday together. He really understood that He had Me on the inside of him. And when he began to see himself as We see him and to live by My Spirit, he began to understand that he was a Light in this world for many.[35] He learned to trust Us in everything and continued to stay focused on Our Words, and We gave Light to his path.[36]

"I love hearing you talk about him like that," I say with a big smile on my face.

"Your grand-pop got it right," Jesus says. "He knew this life on earth wasn't about him. This life was about being the

---

[32] Joshua 1:8
[33] Hebrews 10:23
[34] Psalm 119:105
[35] Matthew 5:14-16
[36] Proverbs 3:5-6, Psalms 119:105

Light for others, loving others, and showing others who I am, through him. That's what it means to live 'Christ-like. The way you do that is by living through My Spirit within you."

Chapter 26 - God Speaking to You

A tear rolls down my cheek as I feel the love I had for my grandfather grow even more.

A part of me wishes I could speak to him right now, but I am currently walking with The Answer to all of the questions I would have for him. I feel so grateful to have spent so much time with him. I am so grateful to have had a role model like that in my life.

"May I teach you something?" Jesus asks.

Laughing, I respond, "Sure thing! Do you think I could ever say no to you?" Which gets a chuckle out of Jesus.

"When you read My Word," Jesus says, "it's just like I am walking and talking with you — because I am the Word.[1] When you read My word, remember to see the words from the perspective of "this is how much God the Father and I love you." As a result, you'll be rooted and grounded in Our

---

[1] John 1:14

Love for you.[2] You won't need to try to produce love, My Spirit within you will do it for you.[3] You won't need to try to "deny yourself," because Love doesn't seek its own;[4] therefore, My Spirit within you will take care of that for you.

"That's awesome," I say.

"Here's another tip you can use while reading My Word," Jesus says. "When one of the writers is writing to the believers, to the church, they usually will use pronouns like 'our,' 'we,' and 'us.' You can try swapping out those words and substituting 'I,' 'me,' and 'my.' It will help you take more ownership of what's written and it's easier to see The Father and I talking to you.

"Here's an example from the verse about love and fear from a few minutes ago: "For God has not given 'ME' a spirit of fear, but of power and of love and of a sound mind."

"Or what about Galatians 5:22-23, "But the fruit of the Spirit [the result of His presence within 'ME'] is love [unselfish concern for others], joy, [inner] peace, patience [not the ability to wait, but how we act while waiting], kindness, goodness, faithfulness, gentleness, self-control. Against such things there is no law."

We walk for a few seconds in silence as I'm trying to wrap my head around all this. I just can't believe how simple and easy this all really is. Just become rooted and grounded in God's Love by spending time with Him and reading His Word from

---

[2] Ephesians 3:17, Colossians 2:6-7
[3] Galatians 5:22-23, Ezekiel 36:25-27
[4] 1 Corinthians 13:5

the perspective of 'this is how much God loves me'. And as a result, faith works, because faith works by love. And through the faith He has given me, I can become the tree that produces His Fruit, because my identity will be His Love and His Holy Spirit within me.

"You must be careful," Jesus says, "do not let this world determine who you are. Let Us and Our Word determine who you are because We already have.[5] Satan is not happy at all because We have defeated him. If he can keep you from knowing who you are in Me, he can keep you from reigning over him in this life. He can cause you to be sick, fearful, stressed out, worried. He can bring big issues into your life.

"As soon as you and all other believers realize your identity in Me, (who you are and what you have in Me), Satan will have no power over you and you'll be able to produce heaven on this earth because of who I am within you. That's what happens when My Holy Spirit within you becomes your identity."[6] In other words, that's what happens when you begin to see yourself as God and I see you.

"Jesus how do I know?" I ask, trying to soak everything in.

"Remember, We have placed verses in the Bible showing you who you are and what you have because of Our Love for you — because of the finished work of the cross. If you see that through the lens of this is how much We love you, you'll begin to receive those promises.

* * *

---

[5] Romans 12:2
[6] 1 John 5:4, Romans 8:37, 2 Corinthians 3:18, Galatians 5:16-17, Galatians 5:22-23

"It's just like those gifts at Christmas we spoke about earlier. When a gift that you're given is wrapped, it's unknown what's inside until you open. When you open the gift it's reading the Word and understanding it's meaning. Receiving the gift is understanding it in a state of thankfulness.[7]

"When you're thankful, you remain humble, and God the Father gives more grace to the humble.[8] Remember grace in its purest form is our Holy Spirit within you.[9] As a result, faith grows the tree.[10] Apply this process consistently, every day, and you'll begin to see yourself as We see you.[11]

"Oh, the consistency thing, right?" I ask. "Like how it's important to be consistent when I work out."

"Exactly," Jesus says, "and while taking care of the body I gave you is important, I want you to set your mind on heavenly things, not on things of this earth.[12] Remember, your eyes can focus on one thing at a time, your choice to decide where to focus. Focus on My words, as they will bring you peace.[13] Focus on the world's words and they will bring distractions, temptations, fears, etc. Just remember, I'll take care of your needs.[14]

* * *

---

[7] 1 Thessalonians 5:16-18
[8] James 4:6
[9] Acts 2:38
[10] Romans 1:17
[11] Joshua 1:6-8, Psalms 1:1-4, Romans 12:2
[12] Colossians 3:1-3
[13] John 14:27
[14] Matthew 6:25-34

"Remember, I love you. God loves you.[15] We will always be with you (as He points to my heart) because of Our love for you. My Spirit is inside you.[16] Keep your focus on My love for you which you can discover by spending time in My Word. Remember, I am the Word.[17] When you spend time in the Word, you'll be spending time with Me.

"The enemy is waiting to distract you like a lion.[18] But no need to fear, I have overcome the world, and because I have, so have you.[19] Greater is He that is in you, that is in the world.[20] You have complete power and authority over Satan.[21] If you begin to know the promises in My Word, you'll learn how to exercise that authority. Satan's goal is to keep you from knowing who you are in Me.

"When you believed in me, We sealed you with the gift, Our Holy Spirit.[22] We see you as a brand new creation, old things passed away, behold all things have become new. Because of your new spirit you are righteous, in a right standing relationship with God.[23]

"In the Old Testament, the law was given and God demanded righteousness. In the New Testament, under God's Grace aka

---

[15] 1 John 3:1
[16] John 14:23, Ephesians 1:13-14
[17] John 1:14
[18] 1 Peter 5:8
[19] John 16:33
[20] 1 John 4:4
[21] John 17:15, Luke 10:19
[22] Ephesians 1:13-14
[23] 2 Corinthians 5:17

Our Spirit within you, God supplies righteousness as a free gift.

"You are righteous[24], you are blameless, We have forgiven all of your sins,[25] past present and future.[26] You are saved, cleansed by My blood, redeemed[27] (bought back from sin and death with my sacrifice), you are Love, because you have My Spirit within you.

"Remember, when you read my word, I am the Word that became flesh. When you read my word, it's like you're walking and talking with Me, just as we are now. It's like you're getting to know Me and My love for you and as a result, you'll begin seeing yourself how God and I see you."

"That feels like a whole different way to live than how I've been living," I say. "I could see that totally changing my life!"

"And not just your life, but others' lives, too," Jesus says. "Ever think of yourself as a cup, before?"

"Um, not really," I say.

"Well, in some ways you are," Jesus responds. "Let me explain."

---

[24] 2 Corinthians 5:15-21
[25] 2 Corinthians 5:15-21, Romans 5:17, Ephesians 1:4
[26] Hebrews 10:16-18
[27] Ephesians 1:7

Chapter 27 - Overflow

"The purpose of why I've called you is to love God, love Me, and love people in the moment, every moment. And I will help you to do that. The thing is, it's not just for your sake, but for others as well."[1]

"Picture yourself as a cup," Jesus continues. "You're the cup and God's Love for you is the water, and the goal is to get filled with our Love for you every single day. And because our Love is so abundant that it never ends,[2] you can get filled to the point where you're overflowing."[3]

"That's gonna make a mess," I joke.

"A good mess!" Jesus smiles. "Because our overflowing love will eventually make a puddle around the cup. What happens if you have a puddle on the ground around you and someone approaches you?"

* * *

---

[1] John 13:34-35
[2] 1 Timothy 1:14
[3] John 7:38

"They get wet," I say.

"Exactly right," Jesus says. "As you experience Our Love and it overflows out of you, the people in your life will begin to experience it as well. They'll be getting wet from the overflow of your cup. The way you speak, how you act, the choices you make…when it's motivated and fueled by Our Love, it will make an impact on others. That's the most loving thing you can do for other people."

"I hear people say all the time that you have to love yourself first," I say, "is that actually not true?"

"Think of it this way," Jesus says, "If you really knew how much We love you, you'd see that it would be impossible to not love yourself. In Our eyes you are loved, cherished, and incredibly valuable; so much so that the Father sent Me to save you.[4] That's how we see you. Remember, our love for you is super abundant, it never ends. So as you are filled to overflowing,[5] the puddle turns into a pond, then a lake, then an ocean. And there is power in an ocean."

Jesus pauses for a second, and I'm okay to let the silence hang. His words are so powerful, and the love I can feel coming from Him gives me a sense of peace like I've never felt before.

"The key," Jesus finally says, breaking the silence, "is to remember who it is doing the filling. A cup can't fill itself, it just has to be a cup and be in line with the right source. If you want to change the world, it begins with filling up with Our

---

[4] John 3:16
[5] 1 Thessalonians 3:12-13

love for you. Stay connected to the source, and we will fill you up to overflowing. Does that make sense?"

"It does," I respond.

"That reminds me," Jesus says, "when the Pharisees asked me what was the greatest command in the law, this is how I responded:

'You shall love the LORD your God with all your heart, with all your soul, and with all your mind.' This is the first and great commandment. And the second is like it: 'You shall love your neighbor as yourself.' On these two commandments hang all the Law and the Prophets.'[6]

"And I said to my disciples this:

"A new commandment I give to you, that you love one another; as I have loved you, that you also love one another. By this all will know that you are My disciples, if you have love for one another."[7]

"Don't think you have to try to do it on your own, because you can't. Remember, I'll be the one who fills you with love until you overflow:

"Now may our God and Father Himself, and Jesus our Lord guide our steps to you [by removing the obstacles that stand in our way]. And may the Lord cause you to increase and excel and overflow in love for one another, and for all people, just as we also do for you; so that He may strengthen and

---

[6] Matthew 22:37-40 NJKV
[7] John 13:34-35 NKJV

establish your hearts without blame in holiness in the sight of our God and Father at the coming of our Lord Jesus with all His saints (God's people)."[8]

"I get everything you're saying," I say, "but I know myself and I know that I can screw anything up, even something simple. How do I make sure I don't get in my own way with all of this?"

"As abundant as Our Love and grace is,[9] so too is our forgiveness for those who are seeking to follow Me.[10] You start by having a heart for loving God, loving me, and loving people. Then you position yourself to be filled with Our Love by spending time in the secret place in prayer[11], by reading our words[12], and by allowing our Holy Spirit to lead you.[13] That will put you right where you need to be.

"Remember this:

"A new commandment I give to you, that you love one another; as I have loved you, that you also love one another. By this all will know that you are My disciples, if you have love for one another."[14]

"I guess it's all about love," I say.

* * *

---

[8] 1 Thessalonians 3:11-13
[9] 1 Timothy 1:14
[10] 1 John 1:9, Psalms 103:10-14
[11] Matthew 6:5-6
[12] John 14:19-21
[13] John 14:26, Romans 8:14, Galatians 5:16-17
[14] John 13:34-35

"It really is," Jesus says. "And the key there is that you're loving people as I have loved you. When you begin to realize how much I love you, when you truly get a glimpse of the depths of My love for you, then you'll be filled with my love, and eventually it will overflow in the form of love for others."

As he says those last few words I realize where we are.

We're back in front of my house.

Chapter 28 - Fulfilling the Lord's Prayer

I look up at Jesus and smile. My heart just feels so warm; so at peace and at home.

Another tear rolls down my cheek, but this one isn't about missing grand-pop. This one is because I'm starting to understand His Love for me. I feel so grateful for Him.

Jesus looks at me with the most gentle and kind eyes and explains, "You see, when you begin living by the Spirit, aka living by faith in your brand new identity — 'Christ in you,'[1] you'll be fulfilling the Lord's Prayer, which is:

Our Father in Heaven,
   Hallowed be your name.
   Your kingdom come — (The Kingdom is Our spirit within you)[2]
   Your will be done — (when your living by Our Spirit within you, you'll only be able to do The Father's will[3]),

---

[1] Galatians 2:20

[2] Luke 17:20-21

[3] Romans 12:2, John 6:38

On earth AS IT IS IN HEAVEN...[4]

You see, learning to live by My Spirit within you will produce heaven on earth, because of who I am within you.[5]

I don't think I've ever had the kind of clarity I have in this moment. It feels so freeing. I look down at Clark, half-covered in mud, and rub his head. "Ready to go in and get a bath, boy?" I ask.

I look back up to thank Jesus for the conversation, but he's gone. It startles me for a second, but I regain my composure quickly when I hear mom's voice behind me.

"There you are," she says, "You're about five minutes from missing dinner."

"Be right in mom," I say, bummed about the fact that I didn't get a chance to thank Jesus when He was standing right there.

I look around the neighborhood and I don't see any sign of Him, but then one of the last things He said to me comes back into my head.

"Remember, when you read my word, I am the word that became flesh. When you read my word, it's like you're walking and talking with me, just as we are now. It's like you're getting to know me and my love for you and as a result, you'll begin seeing yourself how God and I see you."

And with that I realize that this conversation is far from over.

---

[4] Matthew 6:9-10
[5] Galatians 5:16, Galatians 5:22-23

I want to spend the rest of my life walking and talking with Him.

"Thank you, Jesus," I say, "for my grand-pop, for that conversation we just had, for my family, for Clark, and for dying on the cross for my sins. Thank you for giving me your spirit that lives and dwells on the inside of me. I thank You for leading and guiding me through my words and actions through the power of Your Spirit within me, so I can become the tree that produces Your fruit; as it is in heaven."

In YOUR name, Amen.

IDENTITY VERSES

HOW GOD SEES YOU BECAUSE OF JESUS' SPIRIT WITHIN YOU

Christ in You Identity Verses

There are identity verses spread throughout the Bible, but the verses listed below are a great place to begin.

Christ in you identity verses, simply put, are the verses that tell us how God sees you because of what Jesus has done for you at the cross. God has given you a brand new identity when you've accepted Jesus as your Lord and Savior.

These verses are a great place to start when you're looking to discover how much God loves you and how God sees you.

Recommendations:

- Go through each book one at a time (Romans, Ephesians, etc.) highlighting each "identity verse," then begin reading each book, keeping your eye on the identity verses to see the full context of that specific verse(s)
- Read these from the perspective of "This is how much God loves you" and "This is how God defines you, because of Jesus' Spirit within you."

* * *

Praying in line with these verses may look like this:

Galatians 3:26 — "For you are all sons of God through faith in Christ Jesus."

Father, I thank You for loving me. I thank You for blessing me with the gift of your Spirit within me. I thank You for calling me a son (or daughter) through having faith in Jesus. I thank You for accepting me into your family. Jesus thank You for making this possible for me because of what You did for me at the cross. I love You, in Jesus' name, Amen.

IN CHRIST

Romans 3:24	Romans 8:1	Romans 8:2
Romans 12:5	1 Cor. 1:2	1 Cor. 1:30
1 Cor. 15:22	2 Cor. 2:14	2 Cor. 3:14
2 Cor. 5:17	2 Cor. 5:19	Galatians 2:4
Galatians 3:26	Galatians 3:28	Galatians 5:6
Galatians 6:15	Ephesians 1:3	Ephesians 1:10
Ephesians 2:6	Ephesians 2:13	Ephesians 3:6
Philipp. 3:13-14	Colossians 1:28	1 Thess. 4:16
1 Thess. 5:18	1 Timothy 1:14	2 Timothy 1:9
2 Timothy 1:13	2 Timothy 2:1	2 Timothy 2:10
2 Timothy 3:15	Philemon 1:6	2 Peter 1:8
2 John 1:9		

IN HIM

Acts 17:28	John 1:4	John 3:15-16
2 Cor. 1:20	2 Cor. 5:21	Ephesians 1:4
Ephesians 1:10	Philippians 3:9	Colossians 2:6-7
Colossians 2:10	1 John 2:5-6	1 John 2:8
1 John 2:27-28	1 John 3:3	1 John 3:5-6
1 John 3:24	1 John 4:13	1 John 5:14-15

1 John 5:20

IN THE BELOVED or IN THE LORD
 Ephesians 1:6   Ephesians 5:8   Ephesians 6:10

IN WHOM
 Ephesians 1:7   Ephesians 1:11   Ephesians 1:13
 Ephesians 2:21-22   Ephesians 3:12   Colossians 1:14
 Colossians 2:3   Colossians 2:11   1 Peter 1:8

BY CHRIST
 Romans 3:22   Romans 5:15   Rom. 5:17-19
 Romans 7:4   1 Cor. 1:4   2 Cor. 5:18
 Galatians 2:6   Ephesians 1:5   Philippians 1:11
 Philipp. 4:19   1 Peter 1:3   1 Peter 2:5
 1 Peter 5:10

BY HIM or BY HIMSELF or BY HIS BLOOD
 1 Cor. 1:5   1 Cor. 8:6   Col. 1:16-17
 Colossians 1:20   Colossians 3:17   Hebrews 7:25
 Hebrews 13:15   1 Peter 1:21   Hebrews 1:3
 Hebrews 9:26   Hebrews 9:11-12   Hebrews 9:14-15
 Hebrews 10:19-20   1 John 1:7

BY WHOM or FROM WHOM or OF CHRIST or OF HIM
 Romans 5:2   Romans 5:11   Galatians 6:14
 Ephesians 4:16   Colossians 2:19   2 Cor. 2:15
 Philipp. 3:12   Colossians 2:17   Colossians 3:24
 1 John 1:5   1 John 2:27

THROUGH CHRIST or THROUGH HIM
 Romans 5:1   Romans 5:11   Romans 6:11
 Romans 6:23   1 Cor. 15:57   Galatians 3:13-14

Galatians 4:7
Philipp. 4:13
John 3:17
1 John 4:9

Ephesians 2:7
Hebrews 10:10
Romans 5:9

Philipp. 4:6-7
Heb. 13:20-21
Romans 8:37

WITH CHRIST or WITH HIM
Romans 6:8
Colossians 2:20
Romans 6:4
Romans 8:32
Colossians 2:13-15

Galatians 2:20
Colossians 3:1
Romans 6:6
2 Cor. 13:4
Colossians 3:4

Ephesians 2:5
Colossians 3:3
Romans 6:8
Colossians 2:12
2 Timothy 2:11-12

BY ME or IN ME or IN MY LOVE or IN HIS NAME
John 6:57
John 14:20
John 16:33
Mark 16:17-18
1 Cor. 6:11

John 14:6
John 15:4-5
John 15:9
John 14:13-14

John 6:56
John 15:7-8
Matthew 18:20
John 16:23-24

OTHER SIMILAR IDENTITY VERSES
Matthew 8:17
Matthew 18:18-20
Mark 11:23-24
John 6:40
John 14:23
Galatians 5:1
Colossians 1:13
Titus 3:7
Hebrews 2:18
Hebrews 7:22
Hebrews 9:28
Hebrews 13:8
1 Peter 2:21
1 John 1:9

Matthew 11:28-30
Mark 1:8
Luke 10:19
John 10:10
John 17:23
Philipp. 2:5
Colossians 1:26-27
Hebrews 2:9-11
Hebrews 4:14-16
Hebrews 8:6
Hebrews 10:14
James 4:7
1 Peter 3:18
1 John 2:1

Matthew 18:11
Mark 9:23
John 4:14
John 14:12
Galatians 3:29
Philipp. 2:13
Titus 2:14
Hebrews 2:14-15
Hebrews 7:19
Hebrews 9:24
Hebrews 13:5-6
1 Peter 2:9
1 Peter 5:7
1 John 3:2

1 John 3:14　　　1 John 4:4　　　1 John 4:10
1 John 4:15　　　1 John 5:1　　　1 John 5:4-5
1 John 5:11-12　　Revelation 1:5-6

Appendix 1 - A Movie Called Life

Life is like a movie.

If you were to sell or give tickets to the movie of your life, and there were only 10 tickets available, who would you sell or give them to? Who would you want to see it?

Would you keep all the tickets to yourself because the story of your life is really only about you and for you?

Would you invite others to watch the movie of your life?

What about God?

You probably wouldn't keep all 10 tickets to yourself, right? That seems pointless and selfish. So why do we focus on ourselves as we are creating this movie called Life? Why do we think we're the main character and everyone around us only has a supporting role? There has to be a better way.

We could give the tickets to our movie to others. We could invite friends, family, and famous people to watch and see how our life plays out, hoping they would be impressed and inspired by what they see. But if that was the case, would it start affecting our choices? Would we act in such a way that we were seeking their approval from the story of our life?

We're told in the Bible that we should not seek the approval of others, but that we should only seek God's approval. With that in mind, maybe we should live as if we've given all 10 tickets to the movie of our life to God?

Think about that for a second.

If you devoted all of your tickets to God, completely selling out your movie, aka life, to Him, how would that change things? You'd probably be focused on producing a movie that is pleasing to Him. And because of that, your life would, as a byproduct, be acceptable and pleasing to plenty of others, as well.

Now, some of you may feel like suddenly there was a lot of pressure on you to make your life a good movie if God was the only one in the audience. Thankfully, He provides the perfect solution to that.

The easiest way to ensure we are producing a life that is pleasing to Him is to get out of the director's chair and let Him call the shots. With God as the director, he will guide the plot and the actions by his Holy Spirit. And as you follow His instructions, the movie of your life will be pleasing to Him.

With God as the director, you won't need to worry about pleasing others. In fact, by following his lead you'll be serving others and experiencing the power of His direction through you. Not everyone will approve of all the choices your character makes, but that's okay. You're not trying to please them, you're trying to please Him.

* * *

As you think about how the movie of your life has played out up to this point, and where you want it to go, think about what it would be like if your audience was just God. What if your tickets were completely sold out to Christ and the only approval you were seeking was His.

When you're trying to please God and other people at the same time, doubts can start to creep in. You can start to worry about what others think of you, and the fear of people not liking you or not approving of you will affect how the movie plays out. At the end of the day you can't please everyone, so you'll have to choose. Who am I trying to please with this movie? God or other people?

We're all here on this earth for a short period of time. The credits will roll for all of us sooner or later. The good news is, through the gift of the free will God has given you, you can choose who your movie is for and how it will play out.

If you don't give all of your tickets to God, you won't be fully committing yourself to Him, and as a result you leave the door open to become distracted by the enemy.

Give all of your tickets to God and allow His Holy Spirit within you to direct the movie of your life. In the end you'll know that it was pleasing to Him because He was the one producing it in you.

Appendix 2 - Our Journey on The Bridge

Everyone's journey is different, but all travel on one road.

Picture yourself walking on a bridge over a large body of water. The bridge is the Life of Jesus. By His Life, Death, and Resurrection, He became the bridge that crosses us over the river of sin and death and gives us a straight path to our Father.

Once you became a believer, you stepped up on the bridge from the river of sin and death and began moving away from your past. As a result, you're now on the Bridge walking towards God. The goal is to keep focusing on God's Light ahead of you, no matter how dark it gets around you.

At times it is dark outside and you can begin to hear different voices or thoughts: lusts and desires of this world resulting from prideful nature (thinking of self before God), worry/stress/anxiety, low self confidence and self-doubt, etc. It becomes easy to get distracted, especially if you're unaware of where the voices are coming from.

Understanding God's Word and His Promises, we know none of the above voices or symptoms are from God. If they are not from God, then where are they from?

The enemy comes to steal, kill, and destroy. He will begin to distract and tempt you to get your focus away from God. The goal is to keep your eyes set on the Light of God at the end of the Bridge and never give in and never listen to the voices that are not from God.

The beautiful thing is, God didn't leave us alone. Through Jesus, He gave us the gift of His Spirit that lives and dwells on the inside of us. Although we are walking along the Bridge and distractions/temptations are all around us, we still have the Power of the Holy Spirit on the inside of us. God's Spirit literally lives and dwells on the inside of us. Not only is the Holy Spirit going to guide us through life, He is our own personal Light that can not only Light the way for us, but more importantly will Light the Way for others through us.

If we keep our Focus on God, Jesus, and the Holy Spirit within us, we will have truly denied ourselves because we are focusing on Him. Simply stated, WE ARE where our FOCUS is. Are you focused on yourself? Or are you focused on Jesus?

Some of you may be thinking right now that the idea of focusing on God all the time is too difficult. Maybe you've tried to do that in the past and it hasn't worked out. The key, however, is not for YOU to try harder, it's to realize that it's no longer YOU doing the work at all. It is God working through you.

The goal is to be in a relaxed state flowing with the Spirit. Completely trusting the Lord in every situation and in every area of your life. Staying diligent, believing with your heart, confessing with your mouth, and staying in a state of thanksgiving for God's Word and His Promises. Truly applying the faith He has given you is how you can continue to keep moving in the right direction towards God. As you keep focused on him, you won't be distracted by the temptations set out by the evil one.

Develop the faith He has given you by being in a state of relaxation, flowing with Spirit. Completely trust the Lord in all things, which results in a sense of peace and comfort in Him. Know that it is the bridge that is keeping you from falling in the water, and nothing you yourself are doing.

As a result, denying yourself will be a byproduct of flowing with the Spirit because your focus will be on Him and no longer yourself. Be relaxed and completely at peace knowing He is guiding your way.

It may be dark on the bridge, but stay focused on the light ahead of you. Stop trying and let Him take care of it, because He already has through what He has done at the cross.

Salvation Prayer

Give your life to Jesus, ask God for forgiveness, and begin your relationship with Jesus through the Holy Spirit. Even if you're not sure if you have done this or not, today is the day — tomorrow isn't promised.

God, I come before you today as a sinner. I desire to have an intimate relationship with You. God, I ask you to completely forgive me of all my sins. Jesus, I confess right now that you are my personal Lord and Savior and I give my life to you; today and forevermore. I believe that You were crucified for the forgiveness of my sins and I believe God has raised you from the dead for my justification, which means you now see me as right in Your Holy eyes.

I thank You for forgiving me. I thank You for Your mercy. God, I ask that you fill me with Your Holy Spirit, Jesus' Spirit, and teach me to walk in Your ways.

Thank You for loving me and calling me Your child.

In Jesus' name, Amen.